St. Nikodim of the Holy Mountain

What God Has Done for Our Salvation

Translated by Reader Nathan Williams

*Translated from the 2003 Russian edition
by the publisher,
"Prolog" Kiev*

Printshop of St. Job of Pochaev
Holy Trinity Monastery
Jordanville, NY
2006

Printed with the blessing of Metropolitan Laurus
of Eastern America and New York
First Hierarch of the Russian Church Abroad

ISBN 0-88465-138-X

Printed by the Printshop of St. Job of Pochaev
Holy Trinity Monastery,
Jordanville,
N.Y. 13361-0036

St. Nikodim of the Holy Mountain

Table of Contents

On the Greatness of the Divine Eucharist..6

The Denial of Peter 11

Our Sins and Ingratitude towards God 17

What God has done for our Salvation..21

"Little" Sins...24

Striving for Pleasure..28

The Teaching of the Gospel 32

The War that Christ Began...37

The Evil Nested in Sin 42

The Life of Christ

    1. His Obedience to His Parents...45

    2. His Labors 49

    3. His Love 54

Thoughts on the Parable of the Prodigal Son 60

Our Love for God...64

Pride: A Great Obstacle to Our Salvation 68

The Treatment of Pride 72

Weak Faith..77

Sinning Depending on Last Minute Repentance 81

Two Snares of the Devil..85

The Redemption of Man 89

From the Publishers...94

On the Greatness of the Divine Eucharist

Think of a gift, the value of which becomes clear when three things are combined in you: an awareness of the greatness of the gift; love for the One Who gives the gift to you, and an awareness of the benefits it brings. These three wonderful things reveal the gift bestowed in the Mystery of the Divine Eucharist. God, Who created the world, gave us many things. First, He gave us our own selves, bringing us out of non — existence in order that we might exist in His image and likeness. He gave us His countless creations, both heavenly and earthly — not only the immaterial and spiritual, but also the material — o that we might look after them. He created heaven, earth, and all that is therein for us. Still greater was the gift of the incarnation, in which God the Word united Himself with human nature so as to make men gods by grace.

Of every possible gift, only one gift remained, yet even this the Lord gave to man in the Divine Eucharist. Therein He gave men His Most — holy Body and Precious Blood to eat, that the soul of every man might be deified; in this we receive both riches and blessings. Concerning this mystery the venerable John of Damascus writes: "This Mystery is called a "Receiving" since through it we receive into ourselves the very Divinity of God, and a "Communion" since through it we enter into communion with Christ and are

made communicants both of His flesh and of His Divinity."
In short, this Mystery is an image of the whole economy in
the flesh. It contains in itself the Birth of Christ, His life
among men, His sufferings and death, His descent into
Hades, Resurrection, and Ascension, His sitting at the right
hand of the Father, and His Second Coming. All this is com-
memorated in the Divine Liturgies of Basil the Great and
John Chrysostom. In them are likewise mentioned those
blessed ones who by uniting themselves with Christ in the
Divine Eucharist will receive eternal good things. As
Nicholas Kabasilas says in this regard: "Then these blessed
ones will be united to one another and to Christ, as the
members of a body are united to the head and to one another; even now, communing from one Bread and from one
Cup, they enter into this unity, as the Lord said in His
prayer: *That they may be one, even as We are One* (John,
17:22)."

Thus, nothing that we could ask of our Savior remains
upon receiving that of which we would say with Philip,
Lord, it sufficeth us! (John.,14:8) If, then, we begin to seek out
something better for our lives, He shall say to us: "The
Mystery which I bestowed upon you is the fulfillment of all
good things; I have nothing more than this. I have given you
all good things in this Bread and this Wine." What a gift
beyond all comparison this is! What benefaction, unsur-
passed in any age! Not even the many — eyed Cherubim or
the six — winged Seraphim are able to comprehend it. Thus,
beloved, before taking part in this beneficent gift of God,
should you not offer your whole self in sacrifice to the One
to Whom you offer thanksgiving at the Liturgy? Will you
truly continue to be ungrateful, in spite of these great gifts
which God has given you? What will the angels say of such
ingratitude? What will the saints in heaven say of it, who
have come to know the great love of God? Be ashamed of
the ingratitude which you display during the performance

of the Mystery which is called Thanksgiving (Eucharist). It is called this not only because the Lord, when giving it to us, gave thanks to the Father, as it is written: ... *Jesus took bread, and blessed it... And He took the cup, and gave thanks...* (Matt. 26:26 — 27) — but also because it moves us to give thanks to God for His many benefactions and for the grace which He bestows upon us in this Mystery.

Think, also, about how punishments will correspond in measure to these gifts, if we do not use them as we should. In other words, the greater the benefactions received from God, the greater the punishments that you will receive if you allow these Divine gifts to remain fruitless within you. Promise the Lord, therefore, that you will give your whole self to Him, just as He gives all to you. Show gratitude to Him for this great and immeasurable gift, and ask Him that to all the benefactions He has shown you He add one more: the renewal of spirit and of heart, so that you might clearly perceive His benefactions and give thanks for them accordingly.

Think also, beloved, of the love which God shows for you in the gift of Divine Communion. In this Mystery His love reaches the peak of perfection, as says the Evangelist John: *Having loved His own which were in the world, He loved them unto the end* (John, 13:1). As the heat of a furnace is known by the flames shooting out of it, so also the Lord's love for us is made known in the Mystery of the Divine Eucharist.

How, beloved, can you respond to such love from God? Our Lord desires one thing: to be united with your wretched soul, yet you do not wish to be united with Him, the Benefaction that surpasses all things?! The Creator shows such fervent love, and the dust, such coldness?! The Lord deigns to dwell in you and to make you His home, yet you, the ungrateful creation, slam the door before Him and do not wish to let Him in?! By showing such ingratitude you become like the Hebrews, who in the desert wished for the Egyptian onions and garlic — that is, for fleshly pleasures. What more must God do to overcome your stiffness and inhumanity?

Thus, standing before the greatness of God, acknowledge your miserable condition. Consecrate your whole self to the Lord in this Mystery and allow into yourself the beloved Jesus, Who established this Mystery in His great love in order that therein you might express your love for Him, so that it might be an intermediary between the loving God and you who are loved by Him. What heavenly unity, worthy of all love! Wake up, O brother; be vigilant, and with fear guard yourself against every sin that could defile you. Having communed of the Most — pure Mysteries, say to yourself: "Now I have become a house in which God Himself dwells. How can I now make myself an abode of sin? I have united myself with God; how then can I make my members the members of a harlot? *Shall I then take the members of Christ, and make them the members of an harlot? God forbid"* (I Cor. 6:15). Finally, ask God, in Whom you believe and Whom you love, that in you He increase love, a desire for unity with Him, and fervor of love for Him. As on the Holy Table in the church the Lord sacrifices Himself for your love, so also do you, being bound by His love, offer Him your thoughts and desires, as it is written: *A sacrifice unto God is a contrite spirit* (Ps. 50:18). This sacrifice is almsgiving, the doing of every good work, and the cutting off of the passions, as says the Apostle Paul: *I beseech you therefore, brethren, by the mercies of God, that you present your bodies a living sacrifice, holy, acceptable unto God* (Rom. 12:1). In order to become beloved, you must yourself love, as says the beloved disciple of the Lord: *We love Him, because He first loved us* (I Jn. 4:19).

Think also, beloved, about the good which you receive through the gift of the Divine Eucharist. This gift is called a

"Partaking" since through it we become participants in all good things, and above all of the Kingdom of Christ. Concerning this the venerable Isidore Pelusiote says: "The receiving of the Divine Mysteries is called a "Partaking" since through them we are vouchsafed unity with Christ, becoming participants in His Kingdom." Likewise, St. Gregory the Theologian writes: "The Most — holy Body of Christ heals the sick, preserves the well, and strengthens the infirm. Through it we become more meek when corrected, more patient in work, and more fervent in love for God." Finally, through Divine Communion Christ implants in us the seeds of immortality, as He Himself said: *Whosoever eateth My flesh, and drinketh My blood, hath eternal life; and I will raise him up at the last day* (John. 6:54).

The Denial of Peter

Think, beloved, about the cause of a terrible fall, the denial of Peter; who, though he was the foremost and most zealous disciple of Christ, later denied his Teacher with a curse. Learn, then, from his fall.

The chief reason for the denial of Peter was pride. It was this that made Peter think more highly of himself than of the other apostles, when he said: *Though all men shall be offended because of Thee, yet will I never be offended* (Matt. 26:33). Even when the Lord foretold his fall to him, Peter did not pay attention: *But he spake the more vehemently, If I should die with Thee, I will not deny Thee in any wise* (Mark 14:31). It is pride that made him bold and disdainful of danger, not only when he entered the palace of the high priest, where there were many servants, but also when he sat down together with them to warm himself at the fire. He was so bold because he imagined that it was not for him to fear the devil, but for the devil to fear him. How, then, could he remain unshaken at a moment when he was filled with such great pride? *Pride goeth before destruction, and folly before a fall* (Prov. 16:18).

When Jesus was led before the high priest, His beloved disciple followed after Him. He likewise entered the palace of Caiaphas, but was able to evade the danger of denial, since he did not trust in his own powers and was not daring to the point of foolhardiness. He did not permit pride to enter into his heart, and due to this did not deny the

Teacher. It is precisely due to his humility that he did not say in the Gospel that it was he that followed after Christ. As Blessed Theophylact writes, "he thus hides himself out of humility."

O accursed pride, the beginning and root of every sin, what evil have you not brought upon unhappy man? Woe to you, my brother, if you are bold and trust in your own powers alone. Woe to you if you desire to do anything without the counsel of your spiritual father, who is wiser than you and knows better what is useful for you. *Woe to them that are wise in their own conceit, and knowing in their own sight!* (Isaiah 5:21) Woe to you if you do not think in accordance with Divine Scripture and Tradition, and stubbornly break the commandments given you by your spiritual father. Woe to you if you permit pride to blind you, if you believe that you are somehow important in this world. Do you desire, O unhappy one, to know what you are in actuality? Think of this: before God, as the prophet says, all nations are as drops of water (Isaiah 40:15). Now divide this droplet by the number of all men — the dead, the living, and all those who will live after us — and see what a miniscule particle falls to each of this countless multitude. Look, then: this particle, though it is nothing, is you. Your powers, then, are just as insignificant as you. As you yourself are nothing, so also your powers are nothing. Having accomplished this task, be proud of yourself if you are able. If even after this you think highly of yourself, know that you are very close to falling, as says the most — wise Sirach: *Unless a man hold himself diligently in the fear of the Lord, his house shall soon be overthrown* (Ecclesiasticus 27:3).

Think of how many times you have already come close to falling greatly; how many times did the Lord withhold His aid from you because of your pride? Turn to Him, then, and with your whole heart hate accursed pride, in which is the cause of every fall, as says the venerable John of the

Ladder: *Where a fall has overtaken us, there pride has already pitched its tent* (Step 23, 4). Thus, embrace humiliation and love humility, the source of every virtue. If you cover a piece of paper with zeroes, there will clearly be no other numbers on it besides zeroes. However, if you write other numbers — ones, twos, and threes — before each of these zeroes, the zeroes become significant numbers. The same is true with all the virtues: if they are performed without humility, they remain mere zeroes which have no value. Abba Isaac the Syrian likewise says that, of all the virtues, the grace of God is bestowed only for humility. If you do not humble yourself and become as a little child, you will be unable to enter into the Kingdom of Heaven, as the Lord made clear to us: *Verily I say unto you, except ye be converted, and become as little children, ye shall not enter into the kingdom of heaven* (Matt. 18:3). You ought to be ashamed of having so many reasons to disdain yourself; but instead you, being mindless, desire that others esteem you. Pray, then, to Jesus Christ, Who by His divine glance once enlightened Peter's blindness and gave him to know his mistake (Luke 22:61), that He also enlighten your blindness, so that you might learn what was spoken by the Apostle: *Wherefore let him that thinketh he standeth take heed lest he fall* (I Cor. 10:12).

Think also, beloved, of the carelessness which likewise caused the denial of Peter. He *followed Him afar off* (Matt. 26:58). From these words it is clear that at that time Peter was careless and *lukewarm* (Rev. 3:16). He neither desired to leave his Teacher entirely, nor to follow Him until the end. He desired to remain His disciple, but without subjecting himself to the danger in which he would have found himself, had he fought for his Teacher to the end. In contrast to Peter, John, the beloved disciple, stood not afar off, but near to Christ, and entered into the palace of the high priest not only in order to see the end, but in order, if need be, to die for Him. He loved Christ greatly, and did not wish to depart a single step from Him. Peter did not love as fervently as did John. In his carelessness he denied the Teacher, understanding this only when the Lord looked at him: *And the Lord turned, and looked upon Peter. And Peter remembered the word of the Lord* (Luke 22:61). The carelessness of Peter was similar to the cold weather at the time. The Evangelist John says that *the servants and officers stood there, who had made a fire of coals, for it was cold: and they warmed themselves: and Peter stood with them, and warmed himself* (John 18:18). As Theophan Keramevs says, at that time Peter was truly cold in his love for Christ, and for this reason warmed himself by the flames of the fire of the world and of sin, which the servants of the devil had kindled in order that, having made Peter an apostate, they might mock him. John, however, warm in his love for the Lord, had no need to warm himself at this accursed fire. Truly, carelessness is a great evil. For this reason the venerable Mark the Ascetic very frequently calls it "godless," since it makes men godless and causes them to deny Christ.

Now, beloved, put your heart to the test, and see if there is no vice in it, as there was in that of Peter, and if the light which was given to you by God in the Holy Scriptures, from which you learn of the falsity of the pleasures of this life, has not been extinguished. You wish to follow after Christ, but you simultaneously choose a path which leads you neither to Christ, nor to the possession of the good things of this world. In other words, you search for a path which would be neither wide, nor narrow; which would not affect your passions; on which you, like Peter, could follow after Christ from afar. Peter was conquered by carelessness once, but you are conquered by it every day. Do not condemn Peter for having denied Christ; rather condemn yourself, since although you confess your faith in God by your words, in your deeds you deny Him, as the Apostle Paul writes: *They profess that they know God; but in works they deny Him* (Tit.

1:16). Condemn yourself for having made so many false promises, for your stubbornness, for your pride and self — satisfaction. How many times, denying Christ, have you trusted in your own powers alone and worshiped money as an idol! For this reason the Apostle Paul calls acquisitiveness idolatry (Col. 3:5). Simply put, you prefer mere trinkets to Christ, and for the sake thereof deny Him. For this reason Chrysostom said that "there are many ways to deny Christ" (Third Homily on Anna).

You then, my brother, as you have imitated Peter in sin, likewise imitate him in repentance. For, as said the venerable Nikita Stifat, the falls of the saints are described to us so that we might imitate their repentance. Peter once denied the Lord, and repented thereof for the remainder of his life. St. Clement of Rome, a disciple of Peter, in his epistle recalls one of the latter's traits: whenever he heard the crowing of a rooster, he immediately remembered his denial and wept.

You likewise, as soon as you recall your sins, weep for them and pour out bitter tears. Blessed Jerome says that "prayer softens God's anger, and tears incline Him to mercy." John Chrysostom likewise writes that "as the air becomes clean and transparent after the rain, so also after tears the soul becomes pure and the mind, clear." As Peter awoke, as it were, and remembered his sin upon hearing the rooster, so also do you, upon hearing the Lord calling you to vigilance (Mark 13:37), awake from carelessness, remember your sins, and be vigilant. After his fall Peter offered repentance and taught us not to be arrogant, trusting in our own powers, but to trust in the help of God. He likewise taught us not to despair and to be compassionate towards other sinners. You, also, learn humility from the sins which you have committed, and do not condemn sinners, but be compassionate towards them and exhort them not to give themselves over to despair. When Peter offered sincere repentance, his apostolic dignity was restored to him and he again become the first — leader of the apostles. You, also, after repenting, will likewise be able to receive again the grace of adoption that you had lost, and to again become a son of God and an heir of His kingdom.

Be aware that the reason for all of your falls is carelessness; thus, repent thereof before the face of your Divine Teacher and resolve henceforth to begin a renewed life of zeal. Understand that carelessness is a terrible thing, and that its appearance in you is from the devil. Ask God that He deliver you from your own self, since you are often a worse enemy to yourself than the devil, as it is written: "Those who sin wage war against their own lives."

Our Sins and Ingratitude Towards God

Let us think, beloved, about the great and terrible number of our sins, of which we remember only a small part, forgetting the rest. In order to recall even a few of them we must remember all the places in which we have lived, every year of our lives, and all the people with whom we have had contact. Only then will we comprehend the length of the chain of sins which we have committed, the end of one sin became the beginning of another, so that not one aspect of our swiftly —flowing lives remains which we have not defiled in our negligence. All our senses we made into gates by which death enters into the soul, as says the prophet Jeremiah: *Death has come up through your windows* (Jer. 9:21). We have transformed all the inner powers of our soul into instruments of sin.

There is no evil that we have not committed. We have only not done that which we could not, or for which there was not opportune time: the evil that we were able to do, we did. Our whole will, given to us by God that we might strive toward Him, the fullness of all good things, we have used to house within ourselves all the loathsome things of the world. With what incredible ease we have turned from God — as though neither divine nor natural law meant anything to us!

Let us admit to ourselves, my brethren, that in the eyes

of God our whole soul is ailing and covered with wounds, as the body of Job was covered with sores and eaten up by worms. When sin begins to govern a man, that man is punished by death, the fruit of sin. How many times ought we to have been thus punished for all the sins which possess us? If mortal sin can cast us straight into hell, how many times ought we to have been flung there together with our sins? In spite of this, however, in His all — abundant and great mercy the Lord does not reject us, and not only continues to endure us with our sins but even bestows upon us His boundless benefactions. How long will we mock His mercy? Let us therefore confess all the evil we have done and, so far as is possible, imitate God's love. Let us ask Him to punish us for our sins, and promise Him that we will no longer anger Him by our insolent lives. Then He will uphold us by His grace, that we may not fall again into our previous sins, as the most — wise Sirach writes: *O Lord, Father and Governor of my life, leave me not to their counsels, and let me not fall by them* (Ecclesiasticus 23:1).

Let us think also about the burden of our sins, since any one of them is a great and terrible evil — particularly mortal sin, since it wars against the immeasurable goodness of God, and since through it we give offense to God, showing disdain for Him. Any mortal sin is so weighty that neither all the labors of the saints, nor all the sanctity of the Angels, nor all the prayers of the Most — holy Virgin can erase it. On the scales of divine justice nothing can outweigh the burden of one mortal sin, except for the Cross and the Blood of the Savior. Hence, sin is the greatest of all evils.

All the torments of hell cannot be compared with the burden of one mortal sin. Through Sirach the Holy Spirit says that "hell is preferable to a single mortal sin" — so great is the burden of a single serious transgression of the will of God! He who dares to do such a thing has a heart of stone; he is like a dumb beast or a senseless tree. He sins with ease and lack of fear, as though it were not the True, Living God that he wished to hurt, but a god false and imaginary. A Christian who sins and gives offense to Christ with such insolence does that which even idolaters did not dare to do to their false gods of wood and stone.

After all this, what can we do but weep with black tears for the remainder of our lives for the insolence and hardness of heart by which we have given offense to God? In order to please God and to give fitting honor to His greatness, we must resolve to do one very difficult thing, and we must ask the Lord from our whole heart that He give us the power to do this, since without the intervention of divine grace we will be unable to change ourselves. We must fervently entreat the Master Christ that He have mercy upon us, and that he send us sufferings equal in number to the times that we showed ingratitude for His mercy and love by our sins.

Let us think about our ingratitude to God, and about the benefactions with which He responds to it. As soon as we perceive the richness of the good things which the Lord has given us — both things common to all men and things given to each of us individually — we will immediately sense that we are unworthy of all the great benefactions and gifts by which God shows His love for us. What can we then offer the Lord for all that He has done for us? The Angels themselves look with amazement upon the humility, sufferings, and death of Christ, which He took upon Himself for our salvation. We are debtors to the love of God. Inasmuch as He so lovingly suffered and died for us, as though we were the only ones in the world, we are now debtors to His death. Thus, seeing ourselves now surrounded by the many benefactions of God, we must no longer give offense to Him by our sins. Let us continually say the words that the wise Joseph said: *How shall I do this wicked thing and sin against God?* (Gen. 39:9) Why do we anger our Most —sweet Benefactor, Who has bestowed such great gifts upon us?

God created us out of nothing, yet we neglect Him as though He were nothing. In place of God we give preference to our bodies, which are in no way different from rotting stumps. God gave us His life that we might give Him ours also, crucifying our passions and not aggravating His wounds by our sins, as the Apostle Paul also says: *They crucify to themselves the Son of God afresh, and put Him to an open shame* (Heb. 6:6).

The Lord loved us as befits His divine greatness, but we preferred vile pleasures to Him, though they flee from us like shadows. As Blessed Augustine says, "God delivered you from many misfortunes: when you were lost, He directed you to the right path; when you were uncertain, He taught you; when you were sorrowful, He comforted you; when you fell, He lifted you up; when you walked, He guided you; when you came to Him, He received you; when you slept, He watched over you; when you cried out to Him, He bent down to hear you." We, however, have rewarded Him for all this with unheard — of ingratitude.

Let us, then, repent of our insolence and ingratitude, through which we have degraded the goodness of God, and from henceforth with trembling let us fulfill His commandments. Let us confess that we deserve for the earth to swallow us up alive, for the sea to cover us with its waves, for the sun to burn us with its rays, and, finally, for hell to devour us and for eternal torments to engulf us with searing flames.

Nevertheless, while we yet live, all our life may become a time of repentance and of turning to the merciful Lord, Who is always ready to forgive us, to forget our sins, and to grant us unending blessedness in His Paradise.

What God Has Done for Our Salvation

Let us think, beloved, about how much God did in order to save us. First He prepared His Kingdom for all who would be obedient to His will. God did not reserve happiness and blessedness only for Himself, His Son, and the Holy Spirit, but prepared it for us as well, desiring to make us His children by grace and communicants of the Holy Spirit. The heavenly armies, the Archangels and Angels, whose work it is to protect men and help them to save themselves, wage war against the demons for our salvation. Concerning this the Holy Scriptures say that Angels are *ministering spirits, sent forth to minister for them who shall be heirs of salvation* (Heb. 1:14).

For our salvation God created the material world "out of nothing" and set us therein to rule over all His creations, commanding them to serve us, and us to carry out His commands in order to obtain delight in Him in another life. In short, in order that we might be saved, *God hath not appointed us to wrath, but to obtain salvation* (I Thess. 5:9). For our salvation the Lord gave the law and the commandments and sent the prophets, who had no purpose other than to teach us the way of salvation. The Father, the Son, and the Holy Spirit — the whole Trinity works for our salvation. Great as the work of the creation of the world was, equally great, no less, was the work of our salvation. For both our being led into the world and our salvation are the results of the actions of the almightiness of

God. Faith likewise has no purpose other then the salvation of our souls, as the Apostle Peter writes: ... *receiving the end of your faith, even the salvation of your souls* (I Pet. 1:9).

How blind we are, my brethren, if we do not see how much God has done for the salvation of our precious souls. Thus, having now perceived the greatness of salvation, let us live out the few remaining days of our lives, continually remembering the words of the Apostle Paul: *Behold, now is the accepted time; behold, now is the day of salvation* (II Cor. 6:2). After all this, is it possible to never think about what the Lord has done for our salvation? Let us gather ourselves together; let us awaken all our sleeping good inclinations, and let us use the remaining days of our lives for the salvation of our souls. Let us ask what the lawyer asked Christ: "What must I do to inherit eternal life?" "What must I do to be saved?" This is the most essential of all the tasks in the world. Everything else is harmful, useless, and vain. We have already many times endangered our salvation — let us fear to do so henceforth. Let us give thanks to God that in His great goodness He endures our negligence in regard to our salvation. Let us entreat Him that He help us to accomplish the work which we have begun.

Let us think, my brethren, about the labors, sufferings, and death that Christ endured for us in order to save us, and about how, having done this, He showed us that our salvation is what He values most highly. Instead of punishing us for our sins, our insolence, and our continual resistance to His goodness, He suffered for us — for blasphemers and apostates. For the sake of our salvation He did not even withhold His Divinity, but gave it to us. In Himself He united it with human nature and accepted such sufferings that His entire Body, from head to foot, was one great wound. He endured torments such as no man had ever undergone, as the prophet Isaiah also says: *He was a man in suffering, and acquainted with the bearing of sickness* (Isaiah 53:3).

He was born in poverty, in a cave, having no place in

which to lay His head: *The foxes have holes, and the birds of the air have nests, but the Son of man hath not where to lay His head* (Matt. 8:20). In poverty He also died. He endured terrible blasphemies and died a dishonorable death, *and became obedient unto death, even the death of the cross* (Phil. 2:8). In the flesh He received unimaginable tortures from cruel torturers, until His Blood poured out in a stream upon the earth. He underwent sorrows and struggles such as no one has ever undergone — *My soul is exceeding sorrowful, even unto death* (Matt. 26:38). In short, an entire abyss of suffering was poured upon Him in order to extinguish the flame of the eternal torments which we had ignited by our sins, as well as so that we might reach Heaven.

Thus, as God has delivered us from our ruinous condition by such a terrible death, enduring more sufferings than anyone has ever had to endure, let us recognize the value of our salvation. If we do not understand this, how indefensible we shall be before Him!

After all this, let us think, my brethren, about the incredibility of the fact that for our salvation Christ poured out His all — holy Blood, yet we do not wish to look after it as the Apostle Paul commanded: *As we have therefore opportunity, let us do good* (Gal. 6:10). If we do not fear our carelessness now, we will most certainly feel fear before the throne of Christ, the Righteous Judge, when our works are displayed such as they were in actuality.

Let us, then, be ashamed of the irrational and sinful life which we have lived until now, and let us resolve to rid ourselves of all our passions and all the evil which wars against us. If we have neglected our salvation up until now as an insignificant task, unworthy of mention, let us now fervently entreat the Lord that even now He show us how to begin the work of the salvation of our souls, since the time which we could have used for our correction will never return.

"Little" Sins

Let us think about the sins which some call little, which, although not mortal, are nonetheless extremely grave, into which we fall out of weakness and a lack of willpower. A sin which seems little is not so, neither in and of itself, nor in comparison with mortal sins. For instance, a lake may be called small when compared with a vast ocean, though it is in fact not small at all, and contains a great deal of water. So also a small transgression only seems small in comparison with a mortal sin; considered by itself it is a great evil. This is because both great and small sins proceed from the same source — the transgression of divine law, as says the Evangelist John: *Whosoever committeth sin transgresseth also the law: for sin is the transgression of the law* (I John 3:4). Likewise, according to the Apostle James, *Whosoever shall keep the whole law, and yet offend in one point, he is guilty of all* (Jas. 2:10).

And so, my beloved, how can we call our everyday sins little — sins such as falsehood, or when we say: "We will choose the lesser evil, so that a greater does not occur;" sins such as anger, slothfulness in religious piety, envy, the sorrow which we feel when our neighbor becomes better than we; idle talking, carelessness of speech, satiation of the belly, indulgence of the sense of taste, and the like? How can sins which incline us to great evil be called little?

Let us not think, then, that these seemingly petty sins do not oppose the will of God and do not remove us from the divine glory of the Kingdom of Heaven. We are in delusion (prelest') if we think that some widespread sin, such as idle talking, is not a sin in the eyes of God. The Lord said very clearly concerning this: *But I say unto you, that every idle word that men shall speak, they shall give account thereof in the day of judgment. For by thy words thou shalt be justified, and by thy words thou shalt be condemned* (Matt. 12:36). How can we say that our inappropriate laughter is not contrary to the will of God, when our Lord, who became man, not only never laughed, but, in addition to the fact that He wept four times, in His teaching said: *Woe unto you that laugh now! for ye shall mourn and weep* (Luke 6:25). Basil the Great, in his canons for monks, prescribed a week of excommunication for laughter, inappropriate conversations, or joking words: "If anyone should make jokes or laugh inappropriately, let him be excommunicated for one week."

How can we say that overeating, drunkenness, and falsehood are not contrary to the will of God, when the Lord Himself said that He will destroy *all them that speak a lie* (Ps. 5:6), and that the sated shall hunger: *Woe unto you that are full! for ye shall hunger* (Luke 6:25)? Let us consider the following example of how small sins damage virtue and diminish the divine grace that is in us: if a fly falls into fragrant myrrh but is quickly pulled out, the fragrance of the myrrh remains unspoiled; if, however, the fly remains in it, the fragrance turns into stench, as the Holy Spirit said through the mouth of the Ecclesiast: *Pestilent flies will corrupt a preparation of sweet ointment* (Ecclesiastes 10:1).

The same is true for little sins: when a pious and virtuous soul does not cleanse itself of them, they bring it great harm, since if they remain in it for a long time the soul begins to incline its will towards them. The purity of virtue and the fragrance of divine grace are then removed from it, and the attainment of holiness becomes a very difficult thing for such a soul. These sins make the soul impure and odious before God, since if even a single evil thought is impure and odious in the sight of God, as said the writer of Proverbs: *An unrighteous thought is abomination to the Lord* (Prov. 15:26), and if thoughts alone, when they are evil, cut a soul off from God (*Froward thoughts separate from God* — Wisd. 1:3), how much more shall the soul which commits these "little" sins in deed be cut off from the love of God and become repugnant to His boundless grace? It is essential for us to flee these "little" sins; for how can we desire both to please God and to not give up these "little" sins, when nothing could be more odious to Him than this, when we desire to unite Heaven with hell, darkness with light, fire with water, and holiness with evil? These sins, though they seem small, are very grave, since they give offense to the Holy God. Likewise, the greatest possible evil committed against creation is insignificant compared with one that is committed against the Creator. Let us be ashamed of the ease with which we perform acts displeasing to God. Let us fulfill all the commandments of the Lord, without exception, and resolve not to not only commit these little sins, but also to not allow our hearts to be in any way inclined towards them. If we should nevertheless chance to fall into them through the weakness of our nature and will, let us not permit our hearts to become engrossed in them; rather, let us hate, repent, and confess them, asking the Lord to strengthen us by His grace and preserve us from falling into them again.

Let us likewise think about the multitude of evils that "little" sins introduce into our souls. As illness weakens the body, so little sins remove every good work from our soul and weaken it, destroying the virtues that vouchsafe a man the fragrance of holiness. Every sin, even if it seems little, separates us from the fruits of the spiritual life, sets us apart from the Holy Mysteries, and hinders our unification with the Master Christ, as the prophet Isaiah also says: *Your iniq-*

uities separate between you and God (Isaiah 59:2). Every little, forgivable sin makes our soul grow cold in love, kills piety, dries up tears of compunction, extinguishes repentance, and prevents the grace of Christ from coming to dwell within us. However, there is a still greater evil: when, due to little sins, we easily move on to grave, mortal sins, which completely destroy the unhappy man. These sins make powerless the good habits of the soul, and hinder one from receiving help from God.

Let us now look at how we proceed from small to greater sins. It seems an insignificant thing to us to gaze incautiously at someone's beautiful face. But let us observe how sins are born of this The sight of beauty gives impure thoughts an opportunity to attack us; these then begin to draw our attention to themselves. Next, the resolution to procure pleasure appears within us; finally we commit the sin in deed. Repetition of the sin produces a habit; the habit gradually becomes a regular practice; and this practice grows into a need to sin. Such a condition produces despair, and despair plunges a man into eternal torment. The Lord gave the Nazarites a commandment neither to drink wine, nor to eat of the ripe or even the unripe fruit of the vine, nor to drink of their juice. This is because one who eats unripe grapes gradually develops a taste for the ripe, and from this, for grape juice; from this, for wine, and from wine, for drunkenness. We now see how the long chain that began with a "little" sin progresses. One who pays no attention to small sins falls into greater, as the Holy Spirit says through the most — wise Sirach: *He that contemneth small things shall fall by little and little.* (Ecclesiasticus 19:1).

Finally, St. John Chrysostom says that though seeds are small, great trees grow therefrom; likewise, foxes are small creatures, yet they destroy the entire vineyard. So also small passions, like foxes, devour the clusters of the virtues; a man gradually becomes corrupt and from little sins falls into great.

Striving for Pleasure

To obtain pleasure for the five senses is a pleasant and simultaneously torturous aspiration which a man feels in his heart. However, not even the greatest orator could ever fully describe all the evil and harm which pleasure brings to the soul. If the devil should offer us poison, let us not drink it, though he should mix it with the honey of pleasure. (When I speak of pleasures, by these I mean the satisfaction of fleshly lusts — fornication, adultery, and other similar passions.)

Each of us knows that the impurity and shamelessness of pleasures blinds our minds and binds our hearts to the transient things of the world. This shows the words of a certain virtuous man to be true — that, besides infants, few will reach Paradise and be saved. Pleasures feed on much sleep, savory foods, beautiful clothes, a soft bed, and in general all that gives peace to our bodies.

Those who are lovers of pleasure seek after feasts, entertainment, shameless songs, bad company, comedies, and festivals, and do not miss a single opportunity for amusement. Their lives are full of pleasures, fornication, entertainment, and every kind of sin. If anyone reproaches them for such a life, they call him an uncultured peasant who wants to turn the city into a desert and laymen into hermits. This they say in order to justify themselves. They consider only one thing to be good: passing the time with amusements. From the bed they go to the table; from the table, to entertainment; and so their whole life passes, as they run without stopping from one sin to the next: hell opens wide its jaws to swallow them all, and they throw themselves into it. The Lord Himself, through the mouth of the prophet Amos, spoke of how far aristocrats and princes are from happiness, who sleep in soft beds, eat excellent food, and amuse themselves in every imaginable way. Woe to you, O rich, who find rest in this life! Woe to you who sate yourselves with every pleasure! Woe to you who laugh now! Woe to you when men praise and esteem you!

Some will say that entertainments and pleasures are not evil until they crossover the line into sin. Jesus Christ, however, says that such a way of life is a preparation of oneself for torture. Woe to those who for the sake of momentary pleasure shall suffer eternally amid unceasing torments! The Lord forewarned us that the path of pleasure is extremely dangerous. Think of the emptiness that pleasures produce in your soul.

Pleasures and amusements make powerless the strongest man. It is precisely due to them that some Christians become so powerless that upon seeing even the shadow of pleasures and temptations they are immediately prepared to retreat and surrender without a fight. The calling of a Christian is the calling of a soldier. No matter how seductive pleasures may be, they must never conquer the Christian soldier. However, weak soldiers do occur: though they confess the powerlessness that has appeared in them due to fleshly sins, they nonetheless fall into these same sins again.

"Is it truly a sin," you will ask, "to sleep peacefully, to eat and drink well, to go to parties and entertainments?" By this question, however, you only wish to justify yourself: though these are not perhaps sins, through them you nevertheless prepare yourself for sin. All of this prevents you from ever tasting the spiritual good things that come from

God. You will suffer from it just as Solomon once suffered, who was imprudent in pleasures and because of them fell into idolatry, or as the inhabitants of Sodom suffered, who by their gluttony, drunkenness, and love for entertainment reached a terrible and loathsome condition: they fell into debauchery and unnatural vices. Tertullian very often said that Christians must reject pleasures because they pamper a man, and due to this his virtue becomes weak and feeble.

The limpness and weakness that appear in the soul due to pleasures are incompatible with the vocation of a Christian. Our purpose is to become like Jesus Christ, Who is the Head of the elect, as the Apostle Paul teaches us: *Whom He did foreknow, He also did predestinate to be conformed to the image of His Son* (Rom. 8:29). In order to come into His glory, Christ led a life of poverty, sufferings, and abuse; lovers of pleasure fear such a way of life, and for precisely this reason do not wish to repent. Have they found some other Gospel, or has some other Christ come to them and promised the mindless ones beautiful clothes, sweet food, rest, entertainment, and the esteem of men? They have forgotten that *strait is the gate, and narrow is the way, which leadeth unto life.*

Listen to yet another matter of importance. Once a rich and noble magnate who loved pleasure heard of the virtuous life of a certain man, and went to him to ask advice of him. The holy man said to him: "Christ was poor, but you are rich; Christ fasted, but you satiate yourself; Christ had insufficient clothing, but you have clothing in excess; Christ endured sorrows and sufferings, but you eat well, relaxing and sleeping on a soft bed." Upon hearing this, the magnate became distressed and repented, and from that day did not cease to entreat the Lord with tears for forgiveness for the life which he had led. Let this also teach you that it is better to endure sorrows in this life than to suffer eternally in the next. Of this St. Athanasius the Great says: "One who has peace in this world should not hope to receive eternal rest, for the Kingdom of Heaven belongs not to those who live in peace here, but to those who live out this life in sorrows and deprivation" (Sermon on Virginity). Endure in this life, that you may not hear from Christ the terrible words: *Son, remember that thou in thy lifetime receivedst thy good things* (Luke. 16:25). Finally, remember also that the Kingdom of Heaven is acquired not by those who live in idleness and comfort, but by those who take control of themselves, as the Lord said: *The kingdom of heaven suffereth violence, and the violent take it by force* (Matt. 11:12). Thus, say no longer that pleasures are no sin, and turn to God with repentance, that you may become truly happy.

The Teaching of the Gospel

Think, beloved, about how the Teacher of the Gospel is Jesus Christ, the Teacher of all teachers and preachers. He alone is Lord and Teacher, as Nicodemus, who came to Him by night, said to Him: *Rabbi, we know that Thou art a teacher come from God* (John 3:2), and as the Lord said of Himself: *Be not ye called Rabbi, for one is your Master, even Christ* (Matt. 23:8). He came into the world not only to redeem us, but also to teach us, as He Himself says: *For this cause came I into the world, that I should bear witness unto the truth* (John. 18:37).

Likewise, in order to establish this truth more firmly, the Heavenly Father commanded us "with a great voice" to hear this Teacher: *Hear ye Him* (Matt. 17:5). However, let us examine this Teacher more closely. He, unlike other teachers, teaches not so much by word as by action.

Think how many difficult labors our Savior undertook in order to teach us the truth. In order to create all that exists it was enough for Him to say a single word — *He spake, and they came to be; He commanded, and they were created* (Ps. 148:5) — but in order to teach us His will and reveal to us the wealth of His wisdom He put off His greatness and took on the guise of a servant, as the Apostle Paul says (Phil. 2:7). He took on the form of a sinful man, *being in the guise of a man*, and endured all the sorrows that teachers and preachers of the divine word had always undergone.

What more could the Unfailing Truth do for us in addition to revealing Himself to us hypostatically and teaching us the truth? *I am the truth* (John 14:6). In what way could our sweetest Teacher have shown His love for us other than through the labors that He underwent? He climbed mountains and descended them again, and traversed all of Judea on foot; great dishonor came upon Him, men calling Him a glutton, a drunkard, and a demoniac; and all this in order to show us the path that leads to life. *And Jesus went about all Galilee, teaching in their synagogues, and preaching the gospel of the kingdom* (Matt. 4:23).

What answer or justification can you have before the Lord, O sinful man, if you do not believe in His divine teaching and do not walk in His light? *If I had not come and spoken unto them, they had not had sin: but now they have no cloak for their sin* (John 15:22). Be ashamed, therefore, that for so long you followed after the false teachings of the world and of the flesh and neglected the wonderful counsels of divine Wisdom, preferring to follow the counsels of earthly wisdom, which is beastly and devilish; never wishing for anything greater than the glory and respect of men; not trying to heal your senses, your mindless passions and lusts, but rather gathering silver, in order to finally become like an ass laden with money.

You have been given the greatest of gifts: you can hear the Incarnate Word Himself, Whose words prophets and kings desired to hear, and did not: *I tell you, that many prophets and kings desired... to hear those things which ye hear, and have not heard them* (Luke 10:24). When you prepare to read the Gospel and go to open it, do this as though you were opening up Heaven, since this Book, written with great piety, contains within itself the teaching of Christ Himself. St. John Chrysostom wrote thus concerning it: "The reading of the Scriptures is the opening of the Heavens" (Second Sermon on Isaiah). Read it as though the Lord Himself were teaching you. When you read His words, you feel no fear; yet what great fear the hard — hearted Israelite nation felt, and, being unable to endure it, said to Moses: *Speak thou to us, and let not God speak to us, lest we die* (Exodus 20:19).

Contemplate the teachings of this Heavenly Teacher, which are contained in the Gospel, and especially think about His Sermon on the Mount, which the Evangelist Matthew recorded: *Seeing the multitudes, He went up into a mountain ... and He opened His mouth, and taught them* (Matt. 5:1 — 2). Think also about the following three qualities of divine teaching: loftiness, truth, and usefulness. The loftiness of this teaching, which before was hidden and unattainable for wise men, was now made clear, as said the Lord: *I will utter the things which have been kept secret from the foundation of the world* (Matt. 13:35). Until this time the world believed that it would be happy only when it should possess riches, glory, and pleasure. Now you can picture how the human race was amazed when it first heard that the Lord spoke of completely different things — that those who are happy are the poor, those who weep, the humble, the meek, the hungry, the peacemakers, the pure in heart, and the wrongly persecuted and accused; and that, on the contrary, the unhappy are the rich, whose hearts cleave to the good things of the world, those sated with the pleasures of the world, those who make merry, those who laugh, and those who enjoy the esteem of men. Who then can attain the inexpressible height which is inherent in all the teachings of the divine Gospel?!

The Apostle Bartholomew very accurately called the Gospel simultaneously both small and great — small in its size, great in its contents and in the loftiness of its teaching. According to the words of St. Ambrose of Milan, the Gospel is like an abyss in which we can discover the fullness of gifts, like a sea of spiritual mysteries in which swims the mystical Fish —Jesus Christ, Son of God, Savior   [the acronym "fish" the letters which in Greek spell, Jesus Christ, Son of God, Savior] . Blessed Jerome calls the Gospel an abbreviated Theology; Origen calls it the beginning of all Holy Scripture. If, then, Augustine calls the whole of the Holy Scriptures an encyclopedia of every science, and Basil the Great calls it a forge in which souls are forged and a granary of spiritual herbs, how vastly superior is the Gospel which is in it — the New Testament, renewed by the Blood of the Son of God!

The teaching of the Gospel is true because it proceeds from the lips of the very Wisdom of the Most High, Which is truth, as the most — wise Sirach writes: *I (i.e., Wisdom) came out of the mouth of the most High* (Ecclesiasticus 24:3). Likewise, although all men, from Adam to the end of the world, are shown to be liars, God alone does not lie, always remaining true, as says the Apostle Paul: *Let God be true, but every man a lia*r (Rom. 3:4).

The usefulness of the Gospel is clear from the fact that it contains teachings and knowledge which lead to salvation and life, as it is written: *To give knowledge of salvation unto his people* (Luke 1:77), and again: *The words that I speak unto you, they are spirit, and they are life* (John 6:63), since they contain all the foundations of Christian morality: they show us what is good and what is evil, and they clothe us in a new man, "created after Christ" (compare to Ephes. 4:24).

Now, examine your own deeds. Do you not show by your works that your faith is entirely different? When the Gospel teaches you theoretical truths and the dogmas of faith, you acknowledge their great worth; however, when it offers you practical counsels for the correction of your disposition, all of your lusts awaken within you and begin to weigh upon you, not wishing to submit to the commandments of the Gospel. Thus, hearken to what the Lord said: *He that ... receiveth not my words, hath one that judgeth him: the word that I have spoken, the same shall judge him in the last day*

(John 12:48). One must apply one's faith in practice, since theoretically *the devils also believe, and tremble* (Jas. 2:18).

Awake, then, and come to your senses. Kindle anew your faith and love for the Divine Teacher. Repent of having fed your heart until now with deeds contrary to those that the Lord teaches. Pray to Christ that He give you a courageous heart with which you might live in accordance with the words of the Apostle Paul: *Not the hearers of the law are just before God, but the doers of the law shall be justified* (Rom. 2:13).

The War That Christ Began

Think, beloved, about mental warfare, for the sake of which our Lord came into the world, as He Himself said: "I came not to send peace, but a sword" (Matt. 10:34). In this war the Savior Himself, our Jesus, is the Commander and King, great in might and majestic, wise and worthy of love, accompanied by all the angels and the saints. He does not go to war in order to impose His royal taxes upon all the nations subject to Him and thereby enrich Himself; rather, He Himself becomes poor in order to enrich them. Think of Christ as a King Who, amid all the riches of His Divinity and humanity, guides the life of everyone who is obedient to Him. This King of kings and Lord of lords is not only a King, but also a Man, as St. John the Evangelist says concerning this in the Apocalypse: *He hath on His vesture and on His thigh a name written, King of Kings, and lord of lords* (Rev. 19:16).

Then, after this, think of how this King calls all men to battle, including you. He calls us to war with His foes and with our foes, that is, with the flesh, the world, and the devil. In this war the King goes before all the rest, as it is written: *I will go before thee, and will level mountains: I will break to pieces brazen doors, and will burst iron bars. And I will give thee the treasures of darkness, I will open to thee hidden, unseen treasures* (Is. 45:2 — 3). Throughout the whole war He is the first to meet the dangers and to receive the wounds inflicted in battle. Nonetheless, as soon as the war is finished, the glory and the crowns of the victory are given to all the soldiers.

By coming into the world, leading a life of poverty amid reviling and sorrows, and dying the death of the cross, the Lord conquered the world, as He says: *Be of good cheer; I have overcome the world* (John 16:33). He likewise overcame the devil: *Now is the judgment of this world: now shall the prince of this world be cast out* (John 12:31). Finally, He also overcame the flesh, as the Apostle Paul writes: *God [sent] His Son in the likeness of sinful flesh, and for sin, condemned sin in the flesh* (Rom. 8:3). Thus, countless souls triumphantly followed the example of the Lord, and now, having overcome the enemies which we have mentioned, they celebrate the victory with Him in Paradise, where one receives five cities, and another ten, according to the labors of each (Luke 19:11 — 26). O glorious code of war! In earthly wars the soldiers do battle, while the king remains in a safe place; in spiritual warfare the first to enter the battle is the King, the soldiers following after Him.

What, now, must you do when you are called to this war? You see that the war is short, and the victory and rest following it — eternal. You see that the foes whom Jesus desires to overcome are more your foes than His, since Him they are unable to depose from His kingdom, but you they can, if you do not overcome them. Thus, arise and resolve firmly to unswervingly follow after the Lord, to imitate Him in everything, and to undergo everything necessary to please Him. When you become close to Him you will find great happiness therein.

Repent of your former life, which was contrary to the life of Christ, since you had as enemies those who were His friends; that is, poverty and the impoverished, sorrows and the sorrowful, reviling and the reviled. You were like the morning star, who is the prince of the tormented, in contrast to Christ, the Prince of the saved. Thus, switch military camps and in the future have your former foes as friends; likewise, have your former friends as foes, and direct against them your entire spiritual arsenal, in order to gain the victory over them. Also, inasmuch as the victory which follows mental warfare comes from God — as it is written, *A horse is prepared for the day of battle, but help is of the Lord* (Prov. 21:31) — entreat Him that He enlighten you by His grace, so that you might clearly perceive both now and in the future the crosses, sorrows, and deprivations sent to you, and that He give you the strength to endure without a murmur and with thanksgiving, as befits one of His followers, understanding that all trials are valuable and desirable for you; for one who follows after Christ and endures various sorrows in this life will rejoice with his King eternally in the future, as says the divine Paul: *If we suffer, we shall also reign with Him* (II Tim. 2:12).

Think, beloved, about how people who follow after Christ in this war are of three types. The first type includes those who follow after Christ in their thoughts alone, from afar; they are excited by this war, but still are simply unable to resolve to take up arms themselves to do battle against the foe and overthrow him, since they do not desire to imitate the example of Jesus Christ, remaining rather in laziness and idleness.

The second type includes those who arm themselves and enter the fray, but only when they feel a desire to do so; they do only that which seems good to them, not that which is in accordance with the will of God. They think that they can conquer in this war while leading a peaceful life, living according to their own judgment and remaining in pride.

The third type includes those who remain steadfast in spite of all, since they, giving all the powers of their soul and the whole glory of the victory to God, become imitators of Christ. In this war they do nothing without the counsel of their spiritual fathers, always being obedient to their will.

Thus, the first type includes the cold and the idle; the second — the lukewarm and the lazy; and the third — the fervent and the zealous.

To which of these types do you belong, my brother? If to the first, woe to you! For at your Baptism you promised God to wage war with your passions and with the devil, yet you stand idle at a distance instead of taking up arms and going to war. How is it that you have forgotten, unhappy one, that if you do not wage war and conquer here, your enemies will put you to death forever? Do you truly not know that if you do not fight you will receive neither crown nor reward? When has a crown ever been bestowed upon one who remained in pleasures and amusements, as says Basil the Great: "Who, while dreaming, has ever earned a triumphal arch? Or who, while enjoying himself or playing a flute, has been adorned with crowns of victory?" Therefore, beloved, leave off laziness and arm yourself for war against the deadly foes. Do not look at how others fight, so as not to become careless yourself and hear what Moses said to the sons of Gad and Reuben: *Shall your brethren go to war, and shall ye sit here?* (Num. 32:6)

If, however, you belong to the second rank, you are neither fervent nor cold, but lukewarm. To such the Holy Spirit says in the Apocalypse: *So then because thou art lukewarm, I will spew thee out of my mouth* (Rev. 3:16). He will cast you out in the Day of Judgment, when He encounters you who merely talked and did nothing, with the words: *I never knew you: depart from me, ye that work iniquity* (Matt. 7:23). You wish to become virtuous, but without working. You wish to do good, but at the same time you do not wish to offend the world. You strive to be delivered from your evil ways, but do not wish to endure sorrow for the sake of this. You wish to serve God, but only in word. In short, you wish with one glance to take in both heaven and earth. You wish to struggle with the passion to which you are only slightly attached, while not struggling against that which has entirely engulfed you.

When Christ calls you to change yourself, you change only outwardly, without being inwardly reborn. You must not simply fight; you must fight correctly, as says the Apostle Paul: *If a man also strives for masteries, yet he is not crowned, except he strive lawfully* (II Tim. 2:5). Repent, then, of the inconstancy of your thoughts, and henceforth commit yourself into the hands of the Lord, saying from your whole heart: *Lord, I will follow Thee withersoever Thou goest* (Luke 9:57).

The Evil Nested in Sin

God is the perfect good, which we must love; sin is the utmost evil, which we must hate and loathe. God is a measureless depth off perfection, and sin, an abyss of evil. God is a good immeasurably higher than all good things; sin is an evil infinitely more evil than all evils. God is a being compared to Whom all else is nothing; sin is an abomination commensurately foul, in comparison with which all other miseries cannot be called evil. Finally, sin is the greatest monster possible, in both the present and the future lives. God Himself knows of no greater or more terrible monster, which would resist His goodness and greatness. He hates nothing so much as sin (as said the wise Sirach, "Sin is hateful to God"), since if He did not hate it He would not be God. One might also say that hell would cease to be hell if sin were removed from it, and would be transformed into paradise — so potent and bitter is the poison of sin!

What, then, can be said of how loathsome we become before God when we commit sins, which are the enemy of the good God? By thus loving the monster called sin we become evil and repugnant to the Lord Himself. We become hateful to Him, for our sin is hateful to Him, as says the Holy Spirit through the mouth of the most — wise Solomon: *The ungodly and his ungodliness are both alike hateful unto God* (Wis. 14:9).

Let us recognize our woeful position and the depth of our fall. Let us give thanks to the merciful God, Who reaches out to us in order to help us to free ourselves from the loathsome garments in which sin has clothed us.

However, in order for us to be entirely freed from sin, our will must be united with the will of God: only then will our sin be erased. We must use this will together with all our powers to do battle with sin. Likewise, it is essential for us to entreat the Lord to strengthen us by His grace, that we might be able to resist sin and not become enslaved to it.

According to the definition of the venerable Maximus the Confessor, sin is an "unnatural movement" that deprives the unhappy sinner of all supernatural gifts and blessings. It likewise deprives the soul of the grace of adoption — the greatest of the gifts that God has given us. Sin strips the soul naked and brings it down into a most pitiful state of desolation, depriving it of the rewards for good works. In particular it deprives a man of the possibility of being an heir of the Kingdom of Heaven, as says the Apostle Paul: *If children, then heirs; heirs of God, and joint — heirs with Christ* (Rom. 8:17). Sin destroys the blessings given to the soul by God — peace with the conscience and purity of thought. It likewise fills the body with impurity and unbridled lusts; i.e., it destroys the temple of God, as the Apostle Paul writes: *Ye are the temple of the living God* (II Cor. 6:16).

What else can we say? According to St. Athanasius the Great, "Sin and evil came not from God, nor were they in God; they did not originally exist, and have no substance whatsoever." Thus, sin turns a man into nothing. Likewise, Blessed Augustine says: "Evil is nothing other than the absence of good." A man who serves sin lives a life of sorrow and trouble, as did Cain, who when he had killed his brother began to tremble with fear — it seemed to him that the hills swayed and the earth shook, and he therefore called the place in which he had settled "Nod," which means "trembling earth." The life which man lived after the fall cannot be called life, but rather death; or, more precisely, the assurance and the beginning of eternal torment. St. John Chrysostom, in commenting on the twentieth chapter of the book of Genesis, says the following: "A fornicator, an adulterer, or one who serves some other similar sin, even if he should conceal it, finds no peace in life. He fears suspicions, and his soul continually trembles, like shadows in the winter. His sleep is not pleasant; when eating he feels no pleasure; he is filled with fears from which he cannot escape, either by visiting friends or in any other way."

Ultimately, the Christian who is enlightened by word and by faith and who has perceived the evil which sin causes him cannot fall into it again. Let us be ashamed, then, brethren, of the impoverished condition to which sin has brought us, and let us resolve firmly from now on to deal as we should with our bodies which seduce us. Inasmuch as the evil inflicted on us and on God cannot be healed by any other means than by fervent tears, let us entreat Him that He grant us the spirit of true repentance.

Let us think about another evil caused by sin: eternal torment. If we are unable to endure being burned by a small flame for even a minute, with what can the flames of hell be compared? How shall we endure eternal fire? Upon seeing the unspeakable torment of the eternal fire, and being in great fear and ecstasy, the prophet Isaiah said: *Who will tell you that a fire is kindled? Who will tell you of the eternal place?* (Is. 33:14) Let us not forget how terrifying it is to be deprived of the mercy of God, who desires to bestow eternal blessedness upon our souls.

Let us, then, resolve to courageously resist the temptations into which the devil hurls us, so that we may not fall into sin, and let us be ready to sacrifice our life, not once, but a thousand times, only that we might not submit to it. Let us entreat the Lord that He send us His grace, that we also might shed our blood, only that we might not again grieve Him with new sins.

The Life of Christ

1. His Obedience to His Parents

The life of Christ may be examined as three aspects. The first is the obedience that He maintained toward His parents until the age of thirty; the second, His labors during that period of time; and the third, His love for God and neighbor after the age of thirty. Let us consider each of these aspects individually.

Let us think, brethren, about how the Master of all, Whom all that exists obeys, Himself more than all showed obedience to his parents. He obeyed His Most — holy Mother, Who was His Mother by human nature, conceived Him of Her most pure blood, carried Him in Her womb for nine months, and nourished Him with Her milk. He must absolutely have been obedient to Her, being the true Lawgiver of the fifth commandment: *Honor thy father and thy mother, that thy days may be long upon the earth* (Ex. 20:12), and again: *He that is obedient to the Lord shall be a comfort to his mother* (Eccl. 3:6).

He likewise obeyed the righteous Joseph, though He could have not done so, since neither was Joseph His true natural father, nor was the Lord his real son; rather, this fatherhood and sonship were figurative, and not actual. Despite this, however, the Lord maintained complete obedience to them both — both to the real Mother and to the so — called father, as though the latter were His true father. Thus, the Evangelist writes that the Lord ...*was subject unto them* (Luke 2:51).

By His complete obedience to them the Lord fulfilled all the canons and natural laws. Canon 44 of the Counsel of Carthage decreed that children remain subject to their parents until they are able to reason and think rationally; i.e., until they reach the age of fifteen or, still better, twenty, as was established in the thirty — second chapter of the book of Numbers. After attaining this age they are free and can manage their affairs as they see fit. However, Jesus not only fulfilled but doubled the years of obedience which children are obliged to fulfill, and remained subject to his parents for a full thirty years. Thus, the hierarch Gregory of Nyssa, in commenting on the words which the Lord said to His Mother (*Woman, what have I to do with Thee? Mine hour is not yet come* — John 2:4), says that here the Lord, as it were, protests to His Mother that He has not yet attained the age of independence, and wishes rather to continue to be subject to Her. The hour has not yet come for Him to be free and self — governing. Thus, He continues to be obedient to Her and fulfills all that She asks of Him, and turns the water into wine.

Jesus submitted to His parents and obeyed them with all zeal, all joy, and all love, and humbled Himself without the slightest protest and without any outward or inner contradiction. Likewise, He was obedient to them not only in what was easy but also in what was difficult and burdensome; not only in things honorable and glorious, but also in things base and rude.

What indescribable condescension! He Who with His voice summons the clouds and to Whom the rain submits with trembling, as is said in the book of Job: *Wilt Thou call a cloud with Thy voice, and will it obey Thee with a violent shower of much rain?* (Job 38:34) — Him Joseph calls to draw water, and He immediately obeys. He who sends forth the lightening and it immediately goes (*Wilt Thou send lightnings, and they shall go? and shall they say unto Thee, What is Thy pleasure?* — Job 38:35) is called by His Mother to bring wood for the fireplace, and He goes and brings it. He was prepared to obey the will and every request of His parents. He Who said but a single word, and everything came into being (*He spake, and they came to be* — Ps. 148:5), was Himself obedient to every word of His father and Mother when they told Him to prepare dinner, clean the house, or do some other menial task.

What do you say, O reader? If the King of the Angels was obedient to His parents, that is, to dust which He Himself created with His own hands, what obedience ought you to render to your own parents? How ought you to honor them, what love ought you to have for them, and with what consideration ought you to behave towards them? Every child must give his parents these four things which we have mentioned: obedience, honor, love, and consideration. From out of these four others proceed: upbringing, assistance, exhortation, and good example. In particular children must have great patience for the shortcomings which often appear in their parents in old age, as it is written in the Holy Scriptures: *My son, help thy father in his age, and grieve him not as long as he liveth. And if his understanding fail, have patience with him; and despise him not when thou art in thy full strength* (Ecclesiasticus 3:12 — 13).

How, then, do you think to achieve success without heeding the counsels of your parents? Bear in mind what the Word of God says: *A wise son is obedient to his father: but a disobedient son will be destroyed* (Prov. 13:1). If you speak evil of your father, then you are a blasphemer. If you anger and give offense to your mother, then you are cursed of the Lord, for *He that forsaketh his father is as a blasphemer; and he that angereth his mother is cursed of God* (Ecclesiasticus 3:16). If you honor your father, your children will likewise honor you, and if you receive a blessing from your father, the foundations of your home will be firm: *Whoso honoureth his father shall have joy of his own children... For the blessing of the father establisheth the houses of children; but the curse of the mother rooteth out foundations* (Ecclesiasticus 3:5 — 9). In short, it is absolutely essential that you be obedient to your parents. Only if they compel you to do evil and break the commandments of God must you not heed them, preferring love for God. The Lord also, when His parents had been searching for Him while He was in the temple, said to them: *How is it that ye sought Me? wist ye not that I must be about My Father's business?* (Luke 2:49)

And you, my brother — how many times have you disobeyed your parents and your spiritual fathers? How many times have you grieved them by your contradictions? Be ashamed, therefore, of being so far from the example given you by Jesus Christ, Who was a model for you in all the virtues. He was likewise a model of obedience, that you might follow in His footsteps. Repent, ask forgiveness, and entreat Him that He Himself teach you true and perfect obedience. For He, being the Son and Word of God, Who had no need to learn anything, taught us obedience by His example, as says the Apostle Paul: *Though He were a son, yet learned He obedience by the things which He suffered* (Heb. 5:8). Likewise, as He was obedient unto death, *even the death of the cross* (Phil. 2:8), so do you also with all faith and love entreat Him that He strengthen you by His grace, so that you might be obedient to your parents and spiritual fathers until the end, since, as says Basil the Great, "true and perfect obedience has only death as its limit."

2. His Labors

Think, beloved, about how our Lord Jesus Christ, from the time that He became capable of physical labor, did not lead a life of idleness, but worked with His own hands. He was a carpenter, occupied with the working of wood, and built doors and windows and everything else that is made of wood. This He worked at until the age of thirty, and was not only called the son of Joseph the carpenter – as the Evangelist Matthew recounts: *Is this not the carpenter's son?* (Matt. 13:55) — but also simply a carpenter, according the Evangelist Mark: *Is this not the carpenter, the son of Mary?* (Mk. 6:3) While the righteous Joseph was alive, He worked and labored together with him, occupied only by this trade; He helped him in everything, conducting Himself according to the words of the most — wise Sirach: *[He] will do service unto his parents, as to his masters* (Ecclesiasticus 3:7). Just as His parents were poor, eking out their daily living through much work, it was also fitting that the Lord labor together with them, as says St. Basil the Great: "As befitted His youthful age He submitted to His parents, bearing with meekness and good nature all physical labors. That they, though righteous and pious people, were at the same time poor, needy, and not overly rich, is perfectly clear" (Monastic Rule, 4).

After the death of the righteous Joseph, the Lord continued to ply this trade alone. It was not one of the more glorious trades, such as the sciences (physics, geometry, mathematics, music, and the like); rather, it was rough, difficult work, which brought no riches. The Lord worked at this so that He, as a man, might have something to live on, and in order to help His poor Mother and other poor men and strangers. He likewise did this in order to teach men two things: first, to provide an example for all to not sit idly; and, secondly, by His own example to teach men not to despise any trade which, though it be the lowliest and the most inglorious of all, does not hinder a man from attaining salvation. Every working man should remember this; additionally he must refrain from falsehood, swindling, and stealing.

What a wondrous thing! The Master of all, to Whom all things heavenly and earthly submit, Who created all His creations free, humbled Himself to the point of serving men and working whole days for them. The Wisdom that established heaven and earth, and enlightened the human intellect that it might create various arts and trades, humbled Himself to the point of doing rude and difficult work. The Wisdom that with astonishing artistry created heaven and earth, and inspired human thought for the creation of different arts, humbled Himself to the point of engaging in the most humble of these.

It was truly amazing to see Him Who holds the whole world in the palm of His hand rising early in the morning, taking a basket of tools, and going from one task to the next, covered with sweat in the summer and freezing with cold in the winter, and returning home in the evening, weary from work. He Who by His Spirit feeds all that lives, not only animals but even the plants, and fills them with every blessing (*[Thou] fillest every living thing with Thy favor* — Ps. 144:16), worked from morning until night for the wages He needs. The human mind is incapable of comprehending this! No tongue can describe it! At the sight of this the blood runs cold from amazement. Thus, the words which the Lord said were justified: *The Son of man came not to be ministered unto, but to minister* (Matt. 20:28).

You are perplexed and amazed, my brother, when you read of this? Know, then, that the Lord did all this as a wise physician, that by His example He might heal ailing humanity of two sicknesses and passions, by motivating the shiftless and lazy to work and by teaching those who work to conduct themselves honorably, neither stealing from nor cheating their customers. Learn industriousness, therefore, and not from the Angels, but from the Creator of Angels and men Himself.

If you are a patriarch, imitate the true Universal Patriarch, Christ, and remember that it is likewise beneficial for you to work a little: copy manuscripts, or write about something yourself, or occupy yourself with some other spiritual thing, that you may fulfill the duties given you by the decrees of the Church, since by this you will be able to guard your thoughts, to give a good and useful example to the flock, and to fulfill the apostolic commandment which states: *Nether did we eat any man's bread for nought; but wrought with labor and travail night and day, that we might not be chargeable to any of you* (II Thess. 3:8). For whoever does not wish to work, the same ought not to eat, as the Apostle Paul commanded the Christians of Thessalonica: *If any would not work, neither should he eat* (II Thess. 3:10). This the ancient patriarchs likewise did — Chrysostom, Gregory, Athanasius, Cyril, and Eulogius —, and also those who have lived in recent times — Nectarius, Dositheus, Chrysanthus, Jeremiah, and His Holiness Patriarch Sylvester of Antioch, who made a rule for himself to spend three hours each day working at iconography.

If you are a bishop, follow the example of the Great Bishop, as well as that of many ancient and recent bishops. If you are a priest or a monk, it is still more essential that you imitate Jesus Christ by engaging in some work or doing some manual labor. For manual labor, in the words of St. Isaac, is like a muzzle: it prevents idleness from occurring. With the money that you earn you will be able to assist your brethren who are in need.

For this reason all the fathers who are called "laborers," such as John of the Ladder, Ephraim, Isaiah, Everget, and especially Basil the Great (in many sections of his "Rules for Monks"), demonstrate through the Holy Scriptures, by using the example of the Lord, the Apostles, and prophets, that physical labor is very good and useful. Abba Isaac writes thus concerning it: "Relaxation and idleness are destruction for the soul — they provide the demons with an opportunity to harm it." Just as a man has two parts, consisting of both soul and body, so also his work must have two parts. His soul must be occupied with unceasing mental prayer, and his body by labors and handiwork.

If you are rich and well — known, O reader, imitate the One rich in mercy and the *Prince of the kings of the earth* (Rev. 1:5), Who in order to provide you with an example humbled himself so far as to engage in manual labor. Do not permit your riches to lead you into idleness and laziness; rather, work likewise at some small task. You could write books, like the emperor Theodosius, who, after copying out the entire Gospel with his own hand, read it daily, or like the emperor John Cantakuzin, who wrote two excellent books against the Jews and the Muslims. If you have no education, serve others with love (Gal. 5:13): visit the imprisoned, the sick, the widows, and the orphans. Perform deeds of mercy, that you might not be condemned as a lazy and useless servant.

The Lord *took the man whom He had formed, and placed him in the garden of delight, to cultivate and keep it* (Gen. 2:15), not so that he might lazily sit there in idleness. Working with one's hands strengthens the body and makes it sound, while laziness and idleness make it weak, sluggish, and sickly. The most — wise Sirach rightly wrote: *Much evil is learned from idleness.* This we see in actual fact: there are fewer passions and less slyness in one who works, while one who remains idle is often possessed by ferocious passions.

Thus, if you lived a life of shiftlessness and idleness before, awake now at last from the heavy sleep of indolence. Change your life and repent that for so long you have not followed Jesus Christ, but have been like the senseless idols, who have hands, yet never take up anything with them, and feet, but never walk with them. Continually keep in mind the words which one venerable man said at the break of day: "Body! Work, that you may be fed. Soul! Be sober, that you may be saved."

3. His Love

Think, my brother, about how after thirty years the Lord, following His Baptism, possessed perfect love for God and for His neighbor. The venerable Maximus the Confessor says that when the devil heard the voice of the Father calling the Lord His beloved Son (at His Baptism in the river Jordan: *Thou art my beloved Son, in Whom I am well pleased*), he, knowing the two first and greatest commandments of the law (*Thou shalt love the Lord thy God with all thine heart, and with all thy soul, and with all thy might* — Deut. 6:5 — and: *Thou shalt love thy neighbor as thyself* —Lev. 19:18), wished to test the Lord, to see if He truly loved God and neighbor.

After the Lord had been baptized He was led by the Holy Spirit into the wilderness, to the Mount of Temptations. No sooner had the forty days and nights ended, during which He neither ate nor drank, than the devil stood before Him, and as there are three chief passions — love of the flesh, love of glory, and love of money — he began to tempt Him with them. First he tested the Lord to see if He loved the flesh, saying to Him: *If Thou be the Son of God, command that these stones be made bread,* that Thou might eat and appease Thy hunger. But the Lord, preferring love for God to love for this life, responded: *It is written, Man shall not live by bread alone, but by every word that proceedeth out of the mouth of God* (Matt. 4:4).

After this the devil tested the Lord to see if He loved

glory. Permitted by the Lord Himself, he lifted Him up and set Him on a pinnacle of the temple, and said: *If Thou be the Son of God, cast Thyself down*, that men, seeing how He fell to earth and suffered no harm, might glorify Him as a saint and a wonderworker. The Lord, however, preferring love for God and His glory to the glory of men, answered that one must not test God by needlessly asking for a miracle. *Thou shalt not tempt the Lord thy God* (Deut. 6:16).

Finally, the enemy tested whether or not the Lord was afflicted by the love of money. Again he raised Him up, to the top of a high mountain, and in the blink of an eye showed Him all the kingdoms of the world and their glory, and said: *All these things will I give Thee, if Thou wilt fall down and worship me.* But again the Lord, preferring love for God to all the riches and kingdoms of the world, answers the devil: *Thou shalt fear the Lord thy God, and Him only shalt thou serve* (Deut. 6:13). In this manner the Lord, having conquered the three passions, drove away the devil, who departed from Him in shame. *Then the devil leaveth Him, and, behold, angels came and ministered unto Him* (Matt. 4:11).

The tempter, however, was not satisfied with this. Seeing that the Lord had perfect love for God, he again desired to tempt him, this time testing His love for His neighbor. He therefore entered into the hearts of the scribes, the Pharisees, and the high priests and priests of the Jews, and kindled in them a fire of envy and hatred toward the Lord: they began to slander His miracles and to call Him a glutton, a drunkard, and a friend of sinners and tax collectors; likewise, he moved all the Jews to deliver the Lord into the hands of Pilate and to condemn Him to death on the cross.

The Lord, however, knowing all the malice of Satan, having defeated him and driven him from the mountain, gave him no rest, continually distressing him, driving him out of the sick and the possessed and healing the sufferings and infirmities of men who suffered from the sins to which the enemy had urged them. Likewise by His preaching the Lord enlightened the minds of men, which had been darkened by Satan. Despite the fact that the scribes and the Pharisees hated Him, by His meekness and great calmness He brought them over to His side. He greatly loved and pitied them, since they themselves were not so guilty of what they said and did as was the devil, who used them as his tools. Finally, by all the sufferings which He endured, the Lord condemned the devil. Here, on the cross, He showed His perfect love for His neighbor, when He entreated the Father to forgive the sin of those who crucified Him, saying: *Father, forgive them; for they know not what they do* (Luke 23:34). From this it is clear that the Lord loved His neighbor not merely as Himself, but far more, and having perfectly fulfilled the two commandments of love — love for God and love for one's neighbor — He showed the devil that He is the true Son of God, and that in truth, *On these two commandments hang all the law and the prophets* (Matt. 22:40).

But you, my brother — do you really imitate the Lord in this way? Alas! I feel that you are very far from following the example of Jesus Christ, and that you love neither God, nor your neighbor. There are eight signs by which you may learn whether or not you love God as you should. You truly love God if 1) you love Him freely, and not because you are compelled to; 2) you keep His commandments; 3) you love Him from your whole heart, loving nothing so much as you love God; 4) you frequently recall His name, as says Gregory the Theologian: "Those who greatly love someone remember even the name of their beloved with pleasure;" 5) you shed abundant tears when you remember the name of God, as says St. Isaac: "The custom of love is to shed tears at the remembrance of the beloved;" 6) during prayer your mind easily leaves all the cares of the world and cleaves only to the remembrance of God and to love for Him, feeling internal sweetness and peace surpassing all sweetness and all peace, and the more time you spend in prayerful standing before God, the greater your love is for Him; 7) you rejoice when you endure reviling for the love for God and for the fulfillment of His commandments; and 8) your love for God is not defeated by anything else, as says the Apostle Paul: *For Thy sake we are killed all the day long; we are accounted as sheep for the slaughter. Nay, in all these things we are more than conquerors through Him that loved us. For I am persuaded, that neither death, nor life, nor angels, nor principalities, nor powers, nor things present, nor things to come, nor height, nor depth, nor any other creature, shall be able to separate us from the love of God, which is in Christ Jesus our Lord* (Rom. 8:36 — 39).

Thus, test whether all these signs of love for God are present in you. See whether you love God as little children love their parents, or as animals love those who bore them. Do you love God as one loves a benefactor and friend? Is your love directed towards God the way the needle of a ship's compass always points towards north? Test yourself and see whether you keep the commandments of God, since whoever loves God likewise keeps His commandments, as He Himself said: *If ye love Me, keep My commandments* (John 14:15). Conversely, if anyone does not love God, neither does he keep His commandments: *He that loveth me not keepeth not my sayings* (John 14:24). I fear, however, that even if you keep the commandments of God, you do not do so fully, but rather vaingloriously and with thousands of protests.

Test to see whether you love God "with all your soul, and with all your heart, and with all your strength," as He commanded us. For if your love is divided in two by a yearning for something else, though it be as fine as a hair, that has entered your heart, know that you do not love God with your whole soul and with your whole heart. Thus, think about how far removed you are from divine love, the more so because your heart is not divided merely in two, but into many parts.

How terrible is this calling upon the name of the Lord without reverence and in vanity, and that only because you are compelled, perhaps once or twice a day! Your heart is so hardened that not only do you not weep when you hear the sweetest and most beloved name of God — you do not soften even a little when you see God nailed to the Cross and shedding His blood. When you stand in prayer your mind cleaves to every vain and worldly thing; it is here, there, anywhere but on the words of the prayer. If you do stand for a little while in prayer, you quickly become weary and despondent. Behold how little you love God: no sooner do you feel the slightest discomfort than you turn back and forget your former high ideas.

There is yet another important sign of love for God — when you pray for friend and enemy with equal zeal, making no distinction between them. Concerning this St. Gregory Palamas says: "When with compunction and sweet sorrow in your heart you offer prayers to the Lord both for yourself and for every man — both those known to you and those unknown, both friend and enemy, both those who have offended you and those who have not — then know that you indeed love your neighbor with all your soul. Such a condition of soul, however, comes about only when you perform labors of love in secret" (Sermon on the Evangelist John). Finally, concerning how we must love our neighbor as ourselves, in another place the Lord said: *A new commandment I give unto you, that ye love one another* (John 13:34); and not stopping with this, He continued thus: *Greater love hath no man than this, that a man lay down his life for his friends* (John 15:13).

Test also, beloved, whether the signs of true love are to be found in you. For instead of loving your brother, your fellow countryman and co — believer, you hate, hurt, and devour him, as it is written in the epistle to the Galatians: *But if ye bite and devour one another, take heed that ye be not consumed one of another* (Gal. 5:15). Instead of asking forgiveness of God for the sins you have committed, you pray that He punish your offender, like a dog who does not attack the person who has thrown a stone at it, but as an irrational animal runs to and bites the stone itself.

You also do not war against the devil, who by throwing a stone, as it were, incited your brother and made him attack you; rather, being irrational, you turn to attack your brother. You do not love your neighbor more than yourself; you do not even love him as yourself. For while your brother is hungry and thirsty and endures every imaginable deprivation and suffering, you have enough to eat, enough to drink, and something to wear, and are at peace, not even wishing to look upon him. This is contrary to Christian love, as the Apostle Paul writes: *One is hungry, and another is drunken* (I Cor. 11:21).

Thus, repent; change your life, and ask forgiveness of God for having spent it without loving either Him or your neighbor. Likewise, promise Him that from now on you will strive to love both Him and your neighbor, and will compel yourself to do so. Ask Him likewise that He strengthen and preserve you by His grace, thereby renewing the natural powers of love with which He has endowed you.

Thoughts on the Parable of the Prodigal Son

hink, beloved, about how the prodigal son, leaving his father's house, behaved most foolishly. What happened to him when he ceased to be governed by his father? Up until then he had always remained in the embrace of his father, but now he began to do as he pleased. Before, all his father's servants had served him; they all treated him with tenderness, and honored him as the heir of his father's property. He, like his father, was considered master of the house, and had authority over all things.

However, the desire to obtain false freedom made a slave and a hired servant of him, where he had once been a son and an heir. The kingly life that he lived in obedience to his father became burdensome to him. Weariness of this life and a desire for freedom moved him to decide to take his portion of the inheritance and depart from his father's house: *Father, give me the portion of goods that falleth to me* (Luke 15:12). His father did not wish to hinder him in his desire, and released him, that he might know what it meant to be deprived of the blessings that he had at home and disdained, as St. John Chrysostom comments: "The father releases him and does not hinder him from going into a foreign country, in order that he might learn well, from his own experience, what blessings were afforded him by living at home" (First Sermon on Repentance). Inasmuch as his father could not convince him by words, he releases him that he might learn from life and from suffering. Concerning this the aforementioned holy father again says: "God often ceases to teach by words, that man may be taught be life itself," as it is written: *Thine apostasy shall correct thee, and thy wickedness shall reprove thee* (Jer. 2:19). For Adam also, while he was in Paradise, did not value his happiness, but when he was cast out he understood its worth. Thus, the father divides the inheritance between his sons: *And he divided unto them his living. And not many days after the younger son gathered all together, and took his journey into a far country* (Luke 15:12 — 13).

This touching parable, beloved, shows us very clearly an image of the sin that you commit when you depart from submission to God. Was the son richer than you were before you lost your purity? Was he more noble, more beautiful, more glorious than you? All of Paradise was prepared for your inheritance. You were given the grace of adoption, and you were beautiful with the beauty that comes from purity and sinlessness. By the grace of the Holy Spirit you were beloved of the angels, were instructed together with the saints, and were a living temple of God, as says the Apostle Paul: *Now therefore ye are no more strangers and foreigners, but fellow citizens with the saints, and of the household of God* (Ephes. 2:19). This grace was with you always; it guided you and comforted you like a loving mother with heavenly sweetness and the Divine Mysteries. It frequently held you in its embrace as an only child. But you, like this thoughtless youth, disdained all of this, quickly desiring to misuse the freedom given you by God, that you might live according to your own whims. Instead of being obedient to your Heavenly Father and receiving your inheritance in the future, you have departed from Him and become miserable.

How hardhearted you are, preferring creation to the Creator! The easy yoke of the Lord (*My yoke is easy, and my burden is light* — Matt. 11:30) seems burdensome to you, and you consider your captivity freedom. Remove the heavy cloak of darkness and deception from your mind, and learn that there is no freedom other than that which comes from submitting yourself to God and committing yourself to the will of the Heavenly Father, as the Apostle Paul also says: *Now being made free from sin, and become servants to God, ye have your fruit unto holiness, and the end everlasting life* (Rom. 6:22). Let the carelessness under the influence of which you fled from the royal palace become loathsome to you; repent of your mistakes before the Father, and promise Him never to abandon His divine house. Rather, since only a true son may dwell in the father's house, and not a servant such as yourself, pray to the Only — begotten Son of the Father that He make you also a son of the Father, and that He free you from slavery to sin; that you also, as a son, might dwell in the heavenly house of the Father, as He Himself promised: *The servant abideth not in the house forever: but the Son abideth forever. If the Son therefore shall make you free, ye shall be free indeed* (John 8:35 — 36).

Think, beloved, about the miserable life which that poor and unknown youth led outside his father's house, and of what he was deprived. Firstly, he wasted all his inheritance; secondly, he came to live with a very severe master; thirdly, he was given the dirtiest work — looking after pigs — and fourthly, he became so hungry that he wished to eat the pigs' food, but was not even given that. So also every sinner endures the same deprivations and more. Their deprivations are the following: firstly, such an unhappy person loses his friendship with God, and together with this is deprived of heavenly blessings, wasting his mind on the things of the flesh. Secondly, he submits himself to his most bitter enemy — the devil. Thirdly, he forgets the nobility that he received at Baptism. He despises the instruction given him by the Church who nourishes him with her Divine Mysteries. He renounces his adoption by God and plunges himself into the shameful things of the world — into beastly pleasures and fleshly lusts – and wallows like a pig in the muck of these passions. Fourthly and lastly, while in the midst of these foul passions this unhappy person is unable either to be healed or to satisfy his lusts; rather, the more he eats of the food of shameless deeds, the hungrier he becomes. Concerning this blessed Theophylact rightly said: "One who does evil cannot thereby be sated. For pleasure is inconstant; it comes and goes, and the unhappy man is again left empty" (Commentary on the Parable of the Prodigal Son) — a condition truly worthy of tears.

Now, having recognized how greatly you have suffered from sin, how is it that you do not loathe everything evil, which sets you apart from God? Having awakened, why do you not flee from the house of your cruel and inhuman master, who rejoices in nothing so much as your downfall? If you think to find rest by continuing in sin and keeping company with your enemies, know that God and your conscience will not cease to shame and reproach you. How can you then desire both to sin and to remain at peace with your conscience?

Thus, resolve to return to the heavenly house of your Father, acknowledging that away from Him only sickness, sorrow, and deprivation are to be found. By remaining apart from God you are deprived of the blessings that divine grace bestows. If you do not commune of the Most — pure Mysteries, know that you are in a state of insensibility. Thus, so that you might not suffer spiritual hunger and might eternally be filled with the bread of Angels, which is the word of God, remain always with God. In remaining together with Him you will not hunger. You will be able to flee every kind of sin — evil thoughts, murder, adultery, fornication, theft, bearing false witness, and blasphemy — and you will live like a king together with the King of Heaven. Fear not! Rise up from the mud and run to sweetest Jesus, for there is no salvation in any other (Acts 4:12).

Our Love for God

Think, beloved, about the three chief things by which we are induced, or rather compelled, to love God. The first of these is the Lord's command to love Him; the second is the fact that He, more than any other, is worthy of love; and the third is His call for us, through our love for Him, to gain His love for us, which reveals itself in countless benefactions. The first of these commandments is the commandment of love: *Thou shalt love the Lord thy God with all thy heart, and with all thy soul, and with all thy mind. This is the first and great commandment* (Matt. 22:38). It is the first because it is the fulfillment of the whole law and the foundation of Christian morality and perfection, and must hence be the cornerstone of Christian hearts. Love for one's neighbor and every other virtue proceeds from love for God. Every virtue that does not have love as its foundation is founded on hatred. Love is the first of the virtues. This is because love, in contrast to all the other virtues, gives freedom to man, and also because man, if he so desires, can endlessly perfect himself therein. It is the first because it is the "greatest depth" that man can attain. Finally, it is the first because it shall never have an end, but is eternal. For this reason the Apostle Paul said: *Now abideth faith, hope, and love, these three; but the greatest of these is love* (I Cor. 13:13).

Now let us think about how we ought to value this virtue, and with what zeal and attention we ought to cultivate it in ourselves. If the Lord redeemed us that we might love Him, our duty is to entreat Him unceasingly that we be made capable of evincing this greatest of the virtues in deed. How, after He has commanded us to love Him, can we not be attentive to this commandment? What will those tormented in hell wish for but for the fulfillment of this commandment? For as soon as it was proclaimed in hell the tormenting and all — consuming fire would immediately be transformed into the sweet flame of love. Sinners will endure tremendous suffering precisely because they did not love the Lord as He commanded us. They broke His commandments and thereby concealed themselves from His love, as says St. Isaac the Syrian: "With the lash of love those tormented in Gehenna will scourge themselves, who became weakened by sinning against love; they are in the midst of torments greater than any other terrible tortures" (Sermon 84).

In the commandment of love one may see the wondrous humility of the Lord, who commands us to love Him as though He needed our love; yet we remain so insensible that we do not even notice His benefactions. We must choose one or the other, for there is no third option: either we must accept with gratitude the burning love of the Lord, both here and in Paradise, or, rejecting it, we must be burned eternally by the fire of hell. The one flame is saving and life — giving, the other, torturous and lethal. How is it that we mindless ones are unable to understand this, and prefer the murderous fire of hell to the life — giving flame of divine love? The love that we must have for God is described in the following words: *My little children, let us not love in word, neither in tongue; but in deed and truth* (I John 3:18). Our love for God must be above all love for man, as it is written: *Love is strong as death* (Song of Songs 8:6).

Let us repent, therefore, of having sinned against God until now, cleaving more to sin than to Him. Let us angrily drive such impiety away from ourselves, let us love the Lord "with all our soul, and with all our strength, and with all our mind," and let us strive to never allow any sin into our hearts. The Lord induces us to love in many ways — now exhorting us, now terrifying us with the threat of eternal torments. Let us then pray to Him that He grant us the power to love Him, and let us say together with Blessed Augustine: "Thou commandest me to love Thee — grant me that which Thou commandest!"

We must love God more than any other good thing, since in Him is the fullness of all perfection — of beauty, wisdom, holiness, greatness, goodness, eternity, life, peace, freedom, kingship, justice, and salvation. All this is not God, but is rather in God. He Himself is endlessly greater than all of this, as says the venerable Maximus the Confessor: "God Himself is even more infinitely unreachable than that which He is by nature, that which is peculiar to Him, and that which is of Him but outside of Him."

The Lord desires us to allow Him into the best part of our hearts, that we might participate in the aforementioned blessings. If, however, until now we have not loved Him as we ought, let us repent of this, uproot our negligence, and allow Him into the very depths of our hearts. Then will we be able to experience the sweetness of His divine love. Let us weep for the time when we did not love God, since we have lost it forever, and let us say together with Blessed Augustine: "Belatedly have I come to love Thee, the most ancient Beauty; belatedly I have come to love Thee, and, alas! the time when I did not love Thee is already gone." The Lord descended from Heaven in order to kindle this divine fire of love in the hearts of men (*I am come to send fire on the earth; and what will I, if it be already kindled?* — Luke 12:49). Let us pray to Him, therefore, that He enlighten our minds with the knowledge that the most important thing is to love Him; for it is because we do not know that we do not love, as said the divine and irrepressible lover of God, Augustine: "Ignite an eternal light in my soul, that I may feel, know, and love Thee."

The Apostle Paul likewise possessed this love for God, for he says: *Yet [I live not], but Christ liveth in me: and the life which I now live in the flesh I live by the faith of the Son of God, who loved me, and gave Himself for me* (Gal. 2:20). The same was felt by St. Ignatius the Godbearer when he wrote to the Christians in Rome: "I love Jesus, Who gave Himself for me. What shall I render unto the Lord for all that He hath rendered unto me?" and again: "My love has burst into flame. I wish for a drink, for His drink, which is incorruptible love and life eternal."

How can we not love God when He loved us first? *We love Him, because He first loved us* (I John 4:19). He loved us with the same love with which He loves His own Self. His love for us is made the more plain in that by sacrificing His own Son He freed us from the misery of hell, and in place of it granted us the delight of His Kingdom. *For God so loved the world, that He gave His Only Begotten Son* (John 3:16).

Finally, let us not forget that there is nothing in Heaven or on earth so precious as the divine Blood of the Son of God. He shed not a drop of it that the nine ranks of Angels might love Him; but in order that we might love Him, the Lord shed all His blood. How is it, then, that we do not desire to love Him? What bitterness lies concealed in us, if after all the sacrifices that God has made for the sake of our salvation we remain unmoved and indifferent to Him? Let us then repent of our coldness and ingratitude to the Master. From now on let love for Him be the chief foundation of all our actions. God is the God of our hearts, as David says: *O God of my heart... God is my portion forever* (Ps. 72:24). Likewise, let us say together with Blessed Augustine: "O Lord, enslave all my freedom to love for Thee. Take my consciousness, my mind, and my will. Grant me a heart that meditates only on Thy things, thoughts of love for Thee, a consciousness occupied with Thee, and a mind that thinks of Thee."

Pride: A Great Obstacle to Our Salvation

Of all fevers, the most dangerous is the one which is called an "acute" fever, since it is hidden and is thus a dangerous threat to our health. Likewise, of all the passions, which are like fevers of the soul, the most dangerous is pride, for it is as well — concealed as it is destructive in one whom it has stricken. Many, many people not only are not reproached by their consciences for being proud, but become literally drunk with pride; for them it is like an adornment or a wreath. For this reason the prophet Isaiah declares their misfortune unto them: *Woe to the crown of pride, the hirelings of Ephraim... that are drunken without wine* (Isa. 28:1).

Pride is a mindless lust which, when it has possessed a man, suggests to him the idea that he is better than he actually is, and that other people think the same of him as he does. Thus, one who is proud thinks of no one but himself. As a spider sits in the center of its web, so he also puts himself at the center of everything. And as a spider spins the web out of itself, so also one who is proud, whenever he thinks or does anything, considers himself the source of everything. He thinks of servants as dumb beasts, and of their masters as his servants; he behaves towards his relatives as though he did not know them, and treats his countryman like vagabonds and strangers.

The Holy Scriptures perfectly portray the disposition of the proud man in the mindless words of King Nebuchadnezzar: *Is not this great Babylon, which I have built for a royal residence, by the might of my power, for the honor of my glory?* (Dan. 4:27) The self — satisfaction with which he surveyed his kingdom is characteristic of every prideful person. Such a man is especially attentive to how he dresses, as "a peacock preens its feathers as its struts through Babylon." As Nebuchadnezzar admired himself and desired that others likewise admire him, so also every prideful person is not content with praising himself, but desires that others likewise admire and esteem him. If they do not praise him, he considers them his enemies. Likewise, he considers his every merit and talent enormous, like a pauper who, when given a penny, thinks he has been given a gold piece.

The pride of Nebuchadnezzar did not stop at this, however, going even further. He began to boast not only of what was true, but even of what he knew to be false. He maintained that he had built Babylon, when in reality he had only made its walls a little higher and nothing more, the city itself having been built by another king, called Bel.

The prideful behave the same way. They not only boast of and talk about their own deeds, but add obvious lies to this in order to glorify themselves the more and to show that they are better than others. In so doing they go so far as to turn their own shortcomings into virtues. As the mindless Nebuchad-nezzar prattled about great deeds as though he had done them himself, so also the prideful, reproached by their own foolishness, believe that they themselves have attained whatever good is in them, ascribing none of this to God. They have forgotten, in action if not in word, the mindless words of Nebu-chadnezzar, and self — confidently trust in their own powers, particularly industriousness and enthusiasm.

The desolation produced in the soul by pride is indescribable. Think of this: the greatest evil which exists in the world is sin, and the greatest good is divine grace.Now, pride is the root of every sin. It resists the grace of God and inflicts immense evil upon us. It is the worst of all mortal sins, since it easily prompts a man to any one of them. A snake, once it has managed to squeeze its head through a hole, is able to draw the rest of its body through; so also with pride, behind which every possible evil enters into a man, as the Holy Spirit says through Sirach: *Pride is the beginning of sin* (Ecclesiasticus 10:15).

Pride and Christ cannot be present simultaneously in the heart of a Christian: where the one is the Other will not be, and vice versa. It is for this reason that the Lord said to the Pharisees that they, in seeking the glory of men from one another, became unworthy of believing in Him: *How can ye believe, which receive honor one of another, and seek not the honor that cometh from God only?* (John 5:44) From these words you may understand that as soon as glory enters into the soul of a man, faith immediately disappears. How terrible a thing it is that the man who despises the law of God and loves temporal glory instead will be eternally tormented!

This, my brother, is what you are capable of when you are governed by pride. First your soul becomes filled with impurity and passions. Then, as lips full of bad saliva produce dizziness, so also your conscience, filled with the passion of pride, begins to produce uncertainty of faith, particularly regarding the teachings concerning Paradise and hell: you begin to consider them fairy tales. Think about this: divine grace wars with pride. In order for us to participate in this war it is essential that the Lord strengthen us by His grace. He Himself says this: *Without Me ye can do nothing* (John 15:5). The Apostle Paul likewise says: *It is God which worketh in you both to will and to do of His good pleasure* (Phil. 2:13). From this it is clear that it is God who begins and completes every good work in us. Man is not only incapable of completing, but is even unable to begin anything good if he attempts to do so without the assistance of grace. If we wish to be saved we must love God and virtue with all the powers of our soul. Do not forget, my brother, that pride prevents grace from entering our souls; and even if it were to enter it would immediately be driven out.

If a man who is rich in virtue before God allows pride to enter into his heart, he immediately becomes poor, like the Pharisee in the Gospel parable concerning the Publican and the Pharisee. Such a proud person is like a dove that sits in the sun, rejoicing in its purity and its gay plumage, but is then suddenly attacked and killed by a falcon. So also one who boasts of his virtues is immediately carried off by the falcon of the mind – the devil. For this reason the divine fathers wisely said things such as this: "It is both easy and difficult for a man to be saved, because one minute he is raised up to Paradise by his humility, and the next he plunges himself into the torments of hell by his pride and conceit."

Be prudent therefore, my brother, and accept with joy the counsel offered you by the Holy Spirit: *Despise not in thy heart* (Tob. 4:13). Do not permit any sort of pride to possess you – neither inner pride, in the depths of your heart, nor outer pride, in your deeds — for it gives rise to every evil thing that exists in the world, for "in pride there is destruction and great disorder." Humble yourself, therefore, and you will no longer need to fear falls, since God will be continually by your side.

The Treatment of Pride

How can one be cured of the terrible sickness of pride? It enters into us, corrupts us, and makes us impoverished and miserable. It swells us up until we resemble a full wineskin. It deprives us of every virtue, and the words of the most — wise Sirach become applicable to us: *Three sorts of men my soul hateth, and I am greatly offended at their life: a poor man that is proud, a rich man that is a liar, and an old adulterer that doateth* (Ecclesiasticus 25:2). If we think that we can heal ourselves of pride, this is itself the utmost pride. The only way to be healed of pride is to turn to the Lord, and say together with the prophet David: *Let not the foot of pride come against me* (Ps. 35:12). That is to say: O Lord, do not allow accursed pride to set foot on the ground of my soul.

First our mind must be healed, so that we no longer wish to be prideful; after this everything else will be healed. A man's mind is treated by his ceasing to think that he is somehow significant before God and the saints. Earthly glory is a fruit that does not nourish a man, but poisons him. God created the whole world, and in His boundless goodness gave it to men, that receiving it they might glorify the Creator Who reserved all glory and honor for Himself, as the Angels said: *Glory to God in the highest, and on earth peace, good will toward men* (Luke 2:14). If the prideful wish to seize this glory, which belongs to God alone, this is insolence and audacity, and is offensive to the greatness of God. Woe to him who seeks the glory of the world and whom the world considers great! Such glory is vain and empty.

It is vain because it cannot add to or take away anything from us. *If I honor Myself, My honor is nothing* (John 8:54). This means that when a man who has done something begins to glorify himself, this glory is nothingness. Now you see the insignificance of the praise of men, which many seek from the world.

Those who give this glory likewise give it in vain. These do not know that you are sinful and wretched inside; they see only your exterior. What glory can they give you other than the glory that one might give to a beautiful coffin, which is decorated on the outside with inscriptions and epitaphs, but inside is filled with stench and decay, as the Lord said: *Woe unto you, scribes and Pharisees, hypocrites! for ye are like unto whited sepulchers, which indeed appear beautiful outward, but are within full of dead men's bones, and of all uncleaness* (Matt. 23:27). The glory of the world is also vain because it can never compare with heavenly glory. The existence of this whole vulgar world is a mere instant in comparison with eternity. Its glory is vain because it quickly disappears. In comparison with eternity our whole life is less than a heartbeat, less than the blink of an eye, less than an instant.

People esteem you for your beautiful clothes, but by rights such esteem belongs not to you, but to the silkworms of whose threads they are made. No matter how beautifully you may dress yourself, you can never appear lovelier than the peacock with its gold and multicolored feathers, or than the many —colored flowers and lilies of the field. *Even Solomon in all his glory was not arrayed like one of these* (Matt. 6:29), says the Lord. People praise you for your nobility, but this glory belongs to your ancestors, not to you. People esteem you because you are rich, but God knows the multitude of lies by which you acquired your riches, and how they hinder you from reaching Heaven. The Lord said: *A rich man shall hardly enter into the kingdom of heaven* (Matt. 19:23). People praise you for your beauty, but your true charms are hidden beneath your exterior — just as manure is hidden by snow in the winter. Your beauty is short — lived, like snow, and in the end, *"when a man is dead, he shall inherit creeping things, beasts, and worms"* (Eccl. 10:11). If you open any tomb you will be amazed at the falseness of the glory of this world, and that such glory, despite the fact that it is nothing, is so greatly desired in the eyes of foolish people!

Do you now understand, my brother, what human glory is? Now think what the man who seeks it is. If you ask a prophet concerning this, he will tell you that every man — not only the simple, but even those mightier than any king — are essentially nothing, and are filled with infirmity and weakness, ignorance and misery. *All things are vanity, every man living*, says the prophet David. You, my brother, are the same before God. If in addition to this you are proud as well, you are worse than nothing, since you steal the glory that belongs to God alone, as Blessed Augustine said: "Everything good is Thine, O Lord, and Thine is the glory. He that enjoys Thy good gifts, yet seeks glory not for Thee, but for himself, is a thief and a robber; he is like the devil, who desired to seize Thy glory. "Does it not occur to you to humble yourself? Do you not see that in your heart you carry filth and pettiness incommensurable with the Omnipotence of God? If you are proud, you will be punished as a thief who has stolen the glory of God, for He Himself said these words: *I will not give My glory to another* (Isa. 42:8). How destitute you are, O prideful man! Try to find something good that you have done by your own powers. Try, and you will shame yourself, for everything good that you have, you received from God. *What hast thou that thou didst not receive? now if thou didst receive it, why dost thou glory, as if thou hadst not received it?* (I Cor. 4:7)

After the mind of the proud man has been healed of all this, it is likewise necessary to treat his will, driving out of it every desire to boast. This may be accomplished by thinking about how, of all the evils inflicted by pride, the greatest is eternal torment. One must destroy the insensibility with which pride bewitches the heart, and understand one thing: that without humility we cannot be saved: *Except ye be converted, and become as little children, ye shall not enter into the kingdom of heaven* (Matt. 18:3). In the matter of salvation humility is as essential for us as Baptism. What the Lord said of humility He says also of Baptism: "Except a man be born of water and of the Spirit, he cannot enter into the Kingdom of God" (John 3:5). The prophet Isaiah tells us that into hell descend the strong, the glorious, the great, the rich, and others like them: *And the mean man shall be brought low, and the great man shall be disgraced, and the lofty eyes shall be brought low* (Isa. 5:15). Know, my brother, that pride is the standard and battle trumpet of the morning star. The morning star is the prince of all the sons of pride. He is the head of unrepentant sinners, and pride, his chief attribute, is the greatest obstacle to our salvation.

Come to your senses, therefore: examine your inner world, and if you find traces of pride in your heart, strive to wipe them out. Do not condemn a single sinner who is proud of himself, for you yourself know that one who is wicked now can change in a moment, like the thief in the Gospel, and you yourself, though good now, can suddenly turn evil, as occurred with Judas. Indeed, condemnation itself is already a manifestation of pride. The Apostle Paul says: *Who art thou that judgest another man's servant?* (Rom. 14:4). Thus, do not disdain poor and unimportant people, for the poor are the representatives of Christ, as He Himself said of them: *Inasmuch as ye have done it unto one of the least of these My brethren, ye have done it unto Me* (Matt. 25:40).

Do not boast of your nobility and natural gifts, since

even what little you have is not your own, and how many times have you combined them with evil? You are like a Negro who considers white skin a miracle because the only white part of him is his teeth. Do not praise yourself, and do not seek for yourself a place of honor; do not desire to seem better than others, *for that which is highly esteemed among men is abomination in the sight of God* (Luke 16:15). Remember that the Lord can endure your every sin except for pride. Remember the reviling, offenses, and dishonor that Christ endured on the cross, and this will help you to humble yourself.

Weak Faith

Faith is a power that dwells in the mind and the will of a man. The mind is enlightened by heavenly light and contains that which the Lord reveals to it. The will is likewise moved by God to the fulfillment of every good thing that the mind commands it to do. When faith is weak, the mind cannot understand the mysteries of God, and even before the mind understands them the will has no desire to love them. Blessed Augustine said that man can love what is invisible to him, but not what is unknown. This we see in those Christians who consider themselves believers, not because they live according to the teachings of Christ, but only because they were born of Christian parents and were baptized. In actuality they feel the greatness of the Mysteries very little, and know still less of the essence of our faith and how it differs from other religions. In this condition they differ very little from unbelievers.

I now ask every Christian: who are you, that you stand here in the church? Only by your name can I tell that you are a Christian, this being indicated by nothing else. If someone asks you who Christ was, in Whom you believe, it becomes apparent that you are unable to say anything intelligible. Thus, it is correct to say that in our days the faith of Christians has diminished, as the prophet David also said: *Truths have diminished from the sons of men* (Ps. 11:1); for even if they believe in the Mysteries of the Church, their faith is so confused, so cold and weak, that we can confidently say that they know them like the blind man who saw people like trees: *I see men as trees, walking* (Mark 8:24).

God was born in a cave and laid in a manger of dumb beasts in order to teach us not to be enamored of transitory good things. God lived for thirty years in a carpenter's workshop, plying this trade Himself, that we might learn humility. God walked the streets of Jerusalem that He might show us the road leading to Heaven. God suffered on the Cross in order to destroy sin. Yet all of this does not touch the conscience of Christians and does not cause their hearts to tremble. And so I again repeat what I have just said: truths have diminished from the sons of men. Like truth, faith has also diminished among contemporary Christians, for their faith ought not to be simply rules for "what to believe," but also rules for "what to do." It should not merely consist of our believing correctly, but of our living according to our faith: *Faith without works is dead* (Jas. 2:26). Those who confess Christ to be the Teacher of the faith, the Mysteries, and the dogmas that He has revealed to us, nevertheless do not apply His law to their own lives. And though they hear from His lips that blessed are those who suffer for others, who refrain from pleasures, and who forgive the disgraces and offenses inflicted on them, in spite of this they transgress every commandment of God and the divine teaching of Christ, saying in their hearts: "All of this is true in relation to God, but not to the world." Thus these unhappy ones believe that by this they will indeed be justified at the judgment of the incarnate Wisdom of God. The faith of such people is like an amalgam of gold, which in its outward appearance is very similar to real gold, until it is thrown into a fire: then the real gold (if there was any) remains, while the mercury evaporates. So also with these people: they follow after the Divine Teacher only until they have to struggle with the passions. When the time for this arrives they leave Him to Himself. When Jesus Christ commands them to wage war with their passions and overcome them, they immediately renounce His teaching and "turn back."

All evil comes from weak faith. Feebleness and dwindling of faith lead to the destitution of virtue and the enriching of evil. How deprived contemporary Christians are of the great wealth of the virtues that were so abundant in the first centuries of Christianity! Love for God was then so fervent that many Christians of their own free will gave themselves over to the persecutors of the faith for torture; indeed, at times there were not enough executioners to put them all to death. Love for one's neighbor was likewise so ardent in these blessed ones that Clement of Alexandria wrote that he knew Christians who not only sold their property in order to give alms, but even sold themselves into slavery, only that they might be able to help their brothers.

Can the faith of ancient and contemporary Christians be compared? Truly, all contemporary evil comes from weakness of faith. If one cuts the branches from a tree, they may grow back; but if the root is cut the tree quickly dies. What the root is to the tree, faith is to the soul. It nourishes the soul and enables it to grow and bear fruit, and for this reason is called the root of immortality. If a Christian lives, he lives by faith, as says the Apostle Paul: *The just shall live by faith* (Rom. 1:17). Though such a man should come under attack from all the powers of hell, he will easily be able to put them to flight. With the help of faith man achieves perfection in the virtues. If, however, the root of faith is cut, not only do the fruits, that is, the virtues, quickly die, but also the leaves — that by which a Christian is outwardly distinguishable from other people.

When the Apostle Peter was walking upon the water and began to sink, he considered the strong wind the cause of this: *When he saw the wind boisterous, he was afraid* (Matt. 14:30). The Lord, however, told him that the cause was his lack of faith: *O thou of little faith, wherefore didst thou doubt?* So also Christians consider temptations, which cannot not occur, the cause of all their evil deeds and of their evil lives. The true cause of their unseemly deeds is that their faith is poor and weak, for if it were not the devil could not have so terribly enslaved them to sin.

The falcon who is born free, who is accustomed to fly in the pure and open air, and who has tremendous power in his beak and talons — how can he endure being controlled, prodded with a stick, and held in captivity? Will he not defend himself with beak and talon? So also the Christian who knows that sin is repugnant to God and worse than any calamity, and who confesses that the God — man Jesus was crucified in order to destroy sin — how can such a Christian sin? Many Christians think that sin is a childishly innocent evil, and not especially great. They not only consider it a lesser evil, but even make fun of it, some even boasting of the shameful sins they have committed. They are not afraid to sin, and constantly add sin to sin. We, however, just as we would fear to fall asleep at night if there were a snake in our bed, so let us also fear sin, and let us pray to Jesus Christ that He make strong our infirm faith.

Sinning Depending on Last Minute Repentance

In all the world there is no tradesman mindless enough to throw all his goods into the sea and hope that they will return to him. There are Christians, however, who are quite ready to lose their purity of soul and the grace of God — the greatest gifts He has given them – and hope to receive these heavenly gifts back again; i.e., that their former purity will return to them as soon as they make confession. These unhappy ones, though bound by the chains of hell, think that they can cast them off at any time they choose. They walk before the Morning Star, who holds in His hand the keys to their souls, and think that they can freely leave him at any time. I will not describe this delusion further, for it is not new to man. Was it not this that the tempter suggested to Eve when he prompted her to transgress the commandment of God? What was it that he said? *Ye shall not die* (Gen. 3:4); that is, you can do whatever you like, and nothing will happen to you, for God is very kind. Eve was deceived by this, and Adam after her: he "sinned, thinking of divine mercy," which means that Adam fell, believing that he would not really be punished by God, even though God had warned him that he would be.

You then, my brother, what further example do you desire of the greatness of the devil's insolence in his enmity with our Lord Jesus Christ? He, the wretch, went so far as to suggest that the Lord throw Himself from the pinnacle of the temple and expect that the Angels would uphold Him and not allow Him to suffer any evil — as it is written: *Cast Thyself down: for it is written, He shall give His angels charge concerning thee: and in their hands they shall bear thee up, lest at any time thou dash thy foot against a stone* (Matt. 4:6). Thus there is no need to speak of how, by suggesting that same false idea, the enemy has tempted Christians many times, inducing them to throw themselves into various crimes, then add thousands more sins to the first, and still expect that they will someday confess them and be forgiven all by their spiritual fathers. It is amazing that Christians do not notice such an obvious and tangible lie, and that due to this they become completely indifferent to God. They turn confession of sins and repentance, the mercy and goodness of God — the means of our salvation — into the means of their own downfall. Just as a certain poisonous herb called napelon becomes poisonous when covered with dew from heaven, so also these unhappy people turn the saving Blood of Jesus Christ into a lethal poison, since they use this Blood, which after confession ought to wash away and extinguish our sins, to inflame them still more greatly. Can there be anything more criminal than this? What other antidote could be more greatly misused than this, to the great victory and triumph of the devil? St. Ambrose of Milan likewise grieved for this: "The devil sometimes simply exults in our misuse of It."

I am convinced that the majority of Christians are tormented and suffer from this evil and deceitful hope, which nearly plunges them into hell. In spite of the fact that eternal torments are prepared for sinners, they calmly continue to sin, thinking that such torments are fairytales. This is because they think that it is easy to free oneself from sins — one need only tell them to the priest and perform some sort of penance. They think of this, and they feel at ease once again and take no more thought for their sins, thinking that it is still too early for repentance.

The harm that sinners inflict upon themselves in the hope of future repentance consists in their sins becoming still more vile and in their committing them still more frequently. This is because while they have the opportunity to make confession they think that this alone is more than enough repentance to make righteous men of them. Thus these miserable ones are swallowed up by their passions; they cease to restrain themselves in their words and their curiosity, and strain like dumb beasts toward the path of destruction. Who can measure the depth of their fall? Each time that evil desires appear in them and the opportunity presents itself, they immediately fall into sin. Each time an evil thought occurs to them, they throw themselves into lawless acts.

Many sinners who think that their sins are easily forgiven through confession multiply them daily, as much by their evil deeds as by their lusts, shameless conversations, and sinful pleasures, and particularly by causing temptations for others and thereby destroying their souls. In this manner, without noticing it, people who continually think thus can commit thousands of sins. Anyone can see why the righteousness of God opens the gates of hell to such sinners. It is terrible to hear the words that the Lord addresses to them through the prophet Jeremiah: "The treatment has caused you still greater suffering, and has been of no help to you." You are treated, but it does not help. You have made confession repeatedly, and have been granted forgiveness of your sins so that you might destroy them; but instead of this, due to your wickedness, all of this has only caused your sins to multiply. "If I can sin, I can repent as well. I can sin over and over again — after all, I will be going to confession." You are treated, but it does you no good. You make confession the grounds for countless sins, not realizing that this multitude of sins is drawing you down into hell, making you worthy of punishment, as it is written: "The enemy has stricken thee because of the increase of thy sins." In another place, concerning the soul that confesses and cleanses itself of its sins, then sins again and becomes incurable and worthy of being rejected by God, the prophet says: *We would have healed Babylon, but she is not healed: forsake her... for her judgment reacheth unto heaven* (Jer. 51:9).

Great is the harm that sinners inflict upon themselves, expecting to repent in the future, since they sin without shame or fear, and thereby sink still deeper and deeper into the filthy, polluted mire of sin, in the muck of which not even pigs would wallow. They bring harm upon themselves in that they become indifferent to their salvation and begin to despise the commandments of God, as Solomon said: *When the wicked cometh, then cometh also contempt* (Prov. 18:3). When they reach the final degree of wickedness, their mind becomes darkened, their hearts harden, and they never again think of their sins. Some of these not only treat their sins with indifference, but even boast of them as though they were great deeds: as Solomon says, they *rejoice in evils, and delight in wicked perverseness* (Prov. 2:14). Those who say: "If I sin, I will repent and make confession" likewise come to the point of never wishing either to repent or to make confession. Even when they wish to do so they are unable to, since frequent sin has become a habit for them, the habit has become second nature, and their heart has become as hard as a rock: they have become insensitive, and have stifled in themselves all hope of repentance and correction. Thus these miserable ones die — unreformed and unrepentant.

Two Snares of the Devil

The devil sets many different traps to catch human souls and urge them on to their destruction. Two of these are idleness and preoccupation. Both idleness, in which a man sits and rots from laziness, and preoccupation, in which a man is constantly occupied with a hundred different things, are obstacles to salvation. Many Christians sit in idleness for days at a time —they walk the streets of the city, tell each other various bits of news, and discuss the people walking by. If they do go to church, it is only because they have nothing else to do. Thus they spend day after day without any benefit to themselves.

Through the most — wise Sirach the Holy Spirit says: *Much evil has been taught by idleness.* One might say that the devil opened his school of evil and wickedness; then, not wishing to give lessons in evil himself, made idleness take his place as teacher and give the lectures for him. In his school people learn to sin quickly and effortlessly. Everyone there studies sin, but the ones who particularly excel are those whose thoughts are ponderous and slow. There a person learns to sin in thought, desiring in his heart that which he cannot actually do. *Desires kill the sluggard, for his hands do not choose to do anything* (Prov. 21:25). The whole day long he wishes for evil. One who is often lazy cannot commit any evil deed, since he has no wish to do anything at all; in spite of this, however, he plunges into impurity daily in his thoughts.

The thoughts of idle people are an unbroken chain of gossip and condemnation. The more a lazy person neglects his own affairs, the more zealous and industrious he is in discussing the affairs of others. The less he likes to work, the more he enjoys talking with people, which, after all, requires no effort. He can spend whole days in condemnation — even if he is quiet for a short time he soon resumes his foul conversations. Though his lips are sanctified by the Mystery of Baptism, this does not bother him in the least, and he calmly defiles them with condemnation.

As great an enemy as the lazy person is of work, so great a friend is he to pleasures. The idle person is often sorrowful if he does not obtain them. The old saying correctly says that "idle hands are the devil's workshop." Dead — water quickly goes bad; air that does not move quickly becomes harmful; and lazy troops quickly become fatigued. When Great Lent approaches, the lovers of idleness promptly run to their spiritual fathers and under various pretexts beg them to relax the strictness of the fast for them. Let us, however, not give ourselves over to evil and depart from virtue the first time we encounter difficulty.

Thus, idleness is the first snare of the devil. There is another, however: the multitude of various affairs and ambitions with which people burden themselves, giving no peace to their souls.

Like idleness, multitudinous occupations, activities, and concerns give rise to considerable evil. Concerning them, when He spoke of the thorns that choke the seed of the divine commandments and prevent the growth of everything beautiful and good, the Lord said: *And that which fell among thorns are they, which, when they have heard, go forth, and are choked with cares and riches and pleasures of this life, and bring no fruit to perfection* (Luke 8:14). These people, when the time approaches for prayer and for going to church and communing of the Holy Mysteries, have no time for all this, being engrossed in their work. As soon as they cease doing one thing they immediately take up another; yet they have no time to read something beneficial to the soul. They are like a rope that has been tied into thousands of knots that can never be untied. In this way the devil holds captive those who, though they should desire to escape from his hands, can find no way out; and all the while the devil pulls them farther and farther down to earth, finding still more things for them to do, so that they never have time to do good or even to think about it. In this manner everyday tasks and affairs become traps that hold people fast, pull them down to earth, and darken them to such a degree that not a trace of piety remains.

Even if they were to have a little time left over, they would use it for their own affairs. The same thing happens to them that occurs with hunters. A hunter, even when sleeping, dreams that he is awake, hunting for birds and animals that are running from him or becoming caught in his traps. His body is sleeping in bed, but his mind is in the woods. The same thing occurs with those who are possessed by preoccupation. They stand in church and say the words of the prayers with their mouths, but their mind is wandering here and there, thinking about how to best arrange the affairs of their lives. Their thoughts are on how to do one thing or finish another, and no time remains for their souls. Despite the fact that their body is in church, their mind is in the streets. Even when they go to sleep their thoughts run from one task to the next. If you do not like it when you are talking with a friend and he does not listen to you, but instead keeps asking unrelated questions, how can you wish for God to speak to your heart when there is nothing in it but hundreds of empty thoughts?

In order to be delivered from these two afflictions — idleness and preoccupation — pray to the Lord that He enlighten you so that you might understand the purpose for which you were born into the world, as says the prophet David: *O Lord, make me to know mine end, and the number of my days, what it is, that I may know what I lack* (Ps. 38:5). After this, think about how precious your lifetime is. It is so precious that even if all the orators in the world were gathered together they would be unable to describe its full value and significance — there would eventually be nothing left for them to do but lapse, like infants, into silence. But what am I saying? Even if the Angels desired to explain this to us they would be unable to say anything, for the time that God has given us in which to acquire Paradise is as precious as Paradise itself.

Do you now understand the value of the time that the Lord has given us in which to transform our lives? When death suddenly overtakes you, you will search for yet a moment more, but will find none.

There is a story of a certain magnate who for many years was an advisor to his king. When he realized that the end of his life had arrived, he wept bitterly and cried: "Woe is me! I wasted so much paper in writing royal decrees, yet did not find even a minute in which to write down my sins on some useless scrap of paper, so that I might now recall them and repent." You, beloved, may likewise weep at the end of your life for having spent so many years uselessly.

Arise then, and wake from sleep. Be like a pilgrim who, upon lying down to rest, remembers that his companions have gone on far ahead of him, and immediately stands up and continues his journey. Likewise, be *not as fools, but as wise, redeeming the time, because the days are evil* (Eph. 5:15 — 16).

The Redemption of Man

Let us think, beloved, about the ruins in which human nature was lying, and how because of this ruination there remained in human nature no inner strength. Since, as we have already said, any mortal sin is a clear display of disdain for God, no created being can blot out the desolation and evil it inflicts. No man could save us from this condition, since all men were themselves in the same state — enslaved to the devil and loathsome before God because of their sins. The Apostle Paul confirms this, saying: *For all have sinned, and come short of the glory of God; being justified freely by His grace through the redemption that is in Christ Jesus* (Rom. 3:23 — 24).

Not only men but even the Angels were unable to save us. They could neither heal the evil that was in us nor find a way to cure us. They were powerless to give us the eternal blessedness of Paradise. For this reason the prophet Isaiah said: *He became to them deliverance out of all their affliction: not as an ambassador, nor a messenger, but Himself saved them* (Is. 63:9). Who can this be? It is the Son of God and our Lord, who has infinite power and the great wisdom necessary to find a way to free us from the tyranny of the devil, and to give to us all the riches of His Divinity, of grace and glory, making us communicants of His holiness — that is to say, both of His Divinity and of His humanity.

Let us think about how great the despair of human souls was when they, having been sentenced to eternal torment, were the slaves of the demons. The thought of this ought to move us to humble ourselves and give thanks with our whole heart to our Lord Jesus Christ, Who alone was able save us from this unfathomable chaos. We must repent of having up until now forgotten God and the great grace of salvation that He gave us. Let us turn our thoughts to Him — not to an Angel, nor simply to a man — Who gave Himself in order to save us. Let us glorify God for His great gift, which delivered us from eternal torments. Let us pray to Him that He grant us His light, abiding in which we may come to know Him and give thanks to Him together with the Apostle Paul: *Giving thanks unto the Father, Which hath made us meet to be partakers of the inheritance of the saints in light: Who hath delivered us from the power of darkness, and hath translated us into the kingdom of His dear Son* (Col. 1:12 — 13).

Let us likewise think about the height to which the incarnation of God has raised us, concerning which the Apostle Paul says: *When He ascended up on high, He led captivity captive, and gave gifts unto men* (Eph. 4:8). In order to deliver us from eternal torment, God could have simply forgiven us, as might a king who pardons a criminal condemned to death. However, He did not stop at this, which even by itself would have been an indescribable benefaction; rather, He raised us up to Himself by His all — sanctifying grace, and having adopted us as His children made us heirs of all eternal good things. *The Spirit Itself beareth witness with our spirit, that we are the children of God: and if children, then heirs; heirs of God, and joint — heirs with Christ* (Rom. 8:16 — 17).

Who can measure the distance between the chaos that we were in and this height to which the Lord has raised us? Sentenced to hell, we suddenly become able to receive the glory of the Kingdom of God as our inheritance. The Seraphim are amazed at seeing such a transformation, and yet we do not wish to feel this even the least bit in our hearts. The Evangelist John and the Apostle Paul were in rapture at the boundless love of God which was revealed to them, the first saying: *For God so loved the world, that He gave His Only Begotten Son* (Jn. 3:16), and the second: *He that spared not His own Son, but delivered Him up for us all, how shall He not with Him also freely give us all things?* (Rom. 8:32). We, however, do not wish to even think about all this. It is indeed necessary for us to frequently repeat to ourselves the words of the illustrious Dionysius the Areopagite, that God comes out of Himself, moved by His inexpressible love for all His creation and especially for man. He Who is above all comes down to those who are below in order to bestow upon them His goodness. "For the sake of truth we will also dare to say that the One Who is the cause of all, because of His love for the beauty and the good in everything, in the abundance of His loving kindness goes beyond His own Self, being drawn to all that exists by Providence as though by goodness, inclination, and love, and from a condition infinitely exceeding all else is brought down by the super — material power indivisible from Him, which leads Him out" (On the Divine Names, 4:13).

Let us think about yet another great gift that God has given us. He, foreseeing the folly through which we gradually lose all the riches of our salvation that He has given us, and are drawn down from the heights of grace into the abyss of sin, indicated to us the path of repentance by which we shall again be able to return to the grace we had before. For this reason St. Isaac the Syrian called repentance "the grace after grace." How indiscernible is the love of God for mankind! Love such as this is not to be found in men. Yet, despite all this, we remain irrational and insensible. If a person shows us some small sign of love, we immediately thank them. Is not our unheard — of ingratitude to God terrible, which we display when we forget the countless benefactions that He has bestowed upon us? Even the demons do not show such ingratitude, for they, not having received gifts such as ours, once fell from God, and from that time have maintained their apostasy. How grateful we ought to be to the Lord for having shown us such condescension, considering that He punished the fallen angels so severely. God's love for us is so great that no sin of ours can quench it, no matter how great.

Let us likewise think about the means by which God bestowed this great blessing upon us — His divine incarnation. This is the utmost humility, which He took upon Himself, making human nature a participant in His Divinity. David calls this humility a bowing of the heavens: *He bowed the heavens and came down* (Ps. 17:10), while the Apostle Paul calls it abasement: *Who, being in the form of God, thought it not robbery to be equal with God: but made Himself of no reputation, and took upon Him the form of a servant, and was made in the likeness of men* (Phil. 2:6 — 7). Likewise the hierarch Gregory the Theologian, explaining what manner of abasement this was, says: "The Fullness diminishes His glory to the lowest degree so that I, receiving this Fullness, might shine with His glory in full measure" (Homily on the Nativity of Christ). Basil the Great, discoursing on divine condescension and comparing it with the creation of the whole world, notes: "It was God's good pleasure to have compassion on our infirmities, and He was even able to lower Himself to our infirmities themselves. For the preeminence of His power is evinced not so much by the heavens, the earth, the vastness of the seas, the creatures of both water and land, the plants, the stars, the air, the seasons of the year and the various adornments of the universe, so much as by the fact that the uncontainable God could, through flesh, do battle with death, in order that by His own suffering He might grant us passionlessness" (On the Holy Spirit, chapter 8). By taking human nature upon Himself He not only deprived Himself of the glory, blessedness, and peace befitting such an exalted Being as Himself, but suffered primarily from the same things which men suffer in this world — from painful labors, mockery, and torture – and ultimately accepted death on the Cross, as it is written concerning this in the epistle to the Hebrews: ... *who for the joy that was set before Him endured the cross, despising the shame* (Heb. 12:2).

How much the Lord has done for us, enduring for the sake of our salvation a multitude of torments and offenses! Upon seeing this every mind is amazed and every tongue is silenced. The Son of Man had only to say a single word to His Heavenly Father, and help would immediately have come to Him. Instead, however, He desired to free us from the power of darkness, shedding His precious and divine Blood. How can we thank Him for having sacrificed Himself so that we might live forever? Could God have given us anything more than the sacrifice on the Cross, offered by the incarnate Word of God? Has God really required much of us by instructing us to keep His commandments? Of course not. Let us repent, therefore, of our ingratitude toward the God of love. Let us commit ourselves to Him, since He has created us and saved us at such cost. With humility let us ask Him that He burn up the whole of our ingratitude with the fire of His love, so that His Love might shine in us and so that we might love nothing in this world so much as Him. Let us no longer offend Him with our sins, but rather let us serve Him with our whole heart, saying with David: *O Lord, I am Thy servant!* (Ps. 15:7)

From the Publishers

Venerable Nikodim of the Holy Mountain (1749 — 1808) is one of the most well — known Greek saints of recent times. Having received an excellent education he entered monasticism on the Holy Mountain, where he labored in asceticism for many years, fighting for the purity of Church tradition.

The works of St. Nikodim are distinguished by their multifaceted character. From his pen came the collections of patristic works known as the "Philokalia" and "Evergetinos," commentaries on the psalms, the epistles, and the Church canons and liturgical texts; ascetic and polemical works, lives of the Greek New Martyrs, and other works as well.

Of the works of the venerable one, two books are particularly worthy of note: "Unseen Warfare," familiar to the Russian reader in the translation by St. Theophan the Recluse, and "Spiritual Exercises," selected chapters of which are presented in this publication. Catholic publications were the foundations for these books, that of "Unseen Warfare" being the book of the same title by the monk Lorenzo Skupoli, and that of "Spiritual Exercises" being the commentaries of the Italian monk Pinamonti on the well — known book of the same name by Ignatius Loyola, the founder of the Jesuit order. The Greek philosopher E. Phrangiskos, in his treatise on St. Nikodim as the author of these two books, demonstrates that the venerable one did not translate these books himself; their anonymous translation into Greek was given to him by St. Macarius Notaras for correction, supplementation, and revision in an Orthodox spirit. It should be stated that after their revision by the venerable one these books became entirely suitable for the Orthodox reader. Rewritten in easily understandable language and supplemented by many quotes from the works of the Eastern Fathers of the Church, they lost their Latin character. As later became apparent, the original translation of "Spiritual Exercises" from the Latin into Greek was done around 1717 by Emmanuel Romantis, the secretary of the Greek community of the island of Patmos. A striking testimonial to the Latin origins of "Spiritual Exercises" is the abundance of quotations from Latin authors — St. Ambrose of Milan, Blessed Augustine, Blessed Jerome, and others. St. Nikodim's "Spiritual Exercises" was originally published in Venice in 1800, since which time it has been continually reprinted.